Filmmaking Simplified

Practical Techniques for Getting More out of Any Production

Flax Glor

Editor: Andrea Sardella

Cover photo of Charlie Chaplin with crew
is in the public domain.

Author photo by Rae

Library of Congress Cataloging-in-Publication Data is available.

ISBN: 978-1-5377-6683-6

First Edition

DEDICATION

For my parents and grandparents,
who taught me persistence
and always encouraged the
pursuit of my dreams.

CONTENTS

ACKNOWLEDGMENTS

First and foremost, I would like to thank my wonderful wife–along with my friends and family that have shown me nothing but love and support for my Filmmaking and related endeavors over the years–no matter how crazy things have gotten (including the writing of this book).

I would also like to thank all of those that I have been fortunate to work with–or for–and collaborate with (truly too many to name at this point in my career). I'm sure that I have learned something from everybody along the way, whether I realized it at the time or not.

Last but definitely not least, I would like to acknowledge all of those pioneers that have paved the way–both as Filmmakers and Authors. Surely without them, I would not have had the material for this book and would have been lost with nowhere to turn early in my Filmmaking career. Many endured a great deal of adversity to change the standards in an industry that thrives on change yet fears it by nature. Without those that have come before, none of this would have been possible.

INTRODUCTION

Let me preface this by stating that I am not a big-time Hollywood player. I have never directed a hit Movie. I was not born particularly gifted in any aspect of Cinema, and for the first years of my life didn't even seem to notice that one could actually make Movies as an occupation.

My first foray into "experimental" Filmmaking didn't go so well, either. It didn't take long for me to be disallowed to touch the family's 8mm camcorder for several years after shooting some terribly shaky Footage of a hallway that triggered my Mom's vertigo. As a kid, I was under the impression that if one wasn't immediately brilliant at something, they never would be. I didn't understand or appreciate that certain skills take years or even decades of hard work and practice. For years afterward I thought very little about Film or Video, as our camcorder sat on a shelf above my reach, collecting dust.

I happened back upon it thanks to a couple of friends taking a Video Production course our senior year of high school—and caught the bug almost immediately. I knew then what I wanted to do for the rest of my life, only I had no idea how to make that happen. I would discuss it with friends and family, and aside from "move to Hollywood" or go to Film School (both of which I eventually did), I got very little advice otherwise. I had no family or friends in "the business" and no real knowledge yet of how it all really worked.

So, I picked up a book. And I have continued to read various publications (books, magazines, online articles, manuals, etc.) about Filmmaking on a daily basis for the past 20 years. I am a working Filmmaker without a fancy degree or powerful industry connections who has been a part of almost every department on every size Set imaginable. What I have is a mix of both acquired and applied knowledge that I would like to share in a concise and straightforward manner.

This book touches on all aspects of Filmmaking, and can either serve as an introduction for the beginner who can benefit from the wealth of resources listed throughout, or as a refresher for the seasoned Filmmaker to whom I hope to impart some new tools and tricks.

By reading this book, you are making the perhaps first effort on this long path. Malcolm Gladwell's "10,000 Hour Rule" is an accurate prediction of how long it takes to master the craft of making Films. It's not always a smooth journey, but it's a worthwhile one that can last a lifetime if you remain persistent and hungry for constant improvement above all else.

Just a note on the format of the book—it will be introducing a lot of terms and concepts that you may or may not be familiar with. Rather than create a Glossary that would have added significant length to the page count and doesn't suit every learning style, I have decided to use capitalization of these words liberally to emphasize their importance. If you see an unfamiliar term, I encourage you to seek out its meaning and see where that path leads.

To achieve the goals of this book, it was neither prudent nor necessary to go into too much depth on any one subject—but you are welcome and encouraged to take a deeper dive into any or all topics by using the "Suggested Software", "Recommended Reading" and "Online Resources" listed at the bottom of each section (where relevant).

PART 1
SCREENWRITING SIMPLIFIED

Optioning Material

If you are fortunate enough to be in a position where you have the means to Option or Purchase either a Script, Novel or other Intellectual Property (IP), then you will be ahead of the game on the rest of the Screenwriting process and should only need to read the rest of this section for familiarity with what to expect from a hired Screenwriter.

It is wise to pursue every avenue that your connections take you in regards to shopping for the right Source Material, but also make sure that it is a marketable Concept for a Movie. There is some truth to writing about what you know, but most of us don't live that extraordinary of lives, for better or worse. That is, unless everybody that you have ever told your Story to have replied enthusiastically "that should be a Movie!" Likewise, don't bother with the life Story of someone that you happen to know, unless it is genuinely worthy of a Movie. A good gauge is looking at how much other media coverage they have been able to attract with their Story.

Don't go too far into a niche with Source Material that has no Genre equivalent in Movies. Don't waste your time on a Novel if it's only getting lukewarm reviews in the publishing world, unless you have insight in to how to make it significantly better as an adaptation. Remember that Movies must appeal to a wider audience than Books or most other properties because of the substantial financial investment involved in making them.

Optioning material is a contractual process whereby you track down the owner of the Intellectual Property and Purchase the rights for a designated period of time, during which you will be attempting to get your Film made. It can be a high-risk move for a beginning Filmmaker, and

1

one that will most likely yield a lot of skepticism and negative feedback from jaded Writers/content creators. If you demonstrate a genuine passion for their work and have a particular insight that hooks them, you might convince an Author to give you a shot at turning their Story into a Film. Or perhaps you can negotiate a Shop Deal which is a non-exclusive Option. You don't necessarily have to hire a Lawyer to handle all of this, as there are lots of contract templates online. But it can get very confusing without Legal advice so it may be worth it to spend the money at this stage.

Worth mentioning here is Source Material which is always ripe for adaptation can be found in the Public Domain, free and clear of any copyright issues due to when it was created. Perhaps a modern take on an old classic, or a twist on a well-known fable is perfect subject matter for you to develop. Just be absolutely sure that it is in the clear of any ownership issues before developing this Concept.

If you are not in a fortunate enough position monetarily to hire a Writer or Cowriter, or if this is a part of the process that you are particularly passionate about, then you must learn to think like one.

Recommended Reading:
- *The Indie Producer's Guide to Optioning Motion Picture Rights to Books* by Robert Zipser

Online Resources:
- *Filmmaker Magazine* (www.filmmakermagazine.com)
- *Entertainment Law Resources* (www.marklitwak.com)
- *InkTip* (www.inktip.com)
- *The Black List* (www.blcklst.com)

Thinking like a Writer

Writers learn how to view things a certain way, whether it's something interesting they may see on the Television news, to something unique about everyday life, or even a daydream. It's about developing a perspective and staying true to that for the sake of the Story. Our brains are constantly filtering information and telling us what is important and what isn't. If you change the parameters of the input, the output will inevitably be altered. What was a difficult situation when it happened might become a great Story, and one that could help somebody else avoid a similar scenario.

Writing takes practice, just like any skill. More than that, it necessitates developing a certain workflow–one that will allow the project to remain manageable no matter the length or complexity. Most people get overwhelmed by their own lack of knowledge of the process and freeze up at some point. They don't have a roadmap, and they inevitably get lost.

For the beginning Writer/Filmmaker, I am attempting to provide a roadmap, and for the veteran Writer/Filmmaker, perhaps a few new tools to use. This is not about being formulaic by any means, but about having a process that invites rather than inhibits creativity.

Recommended Reading:
- *Big Magic: Creative Living Beyond Fear* by Elizabeth Gilbert
- *The Power of Your Subconscious Mind* by Joseph Murphy
- *The Artist's Way* by Julia Cameron

Online Resources:
- *Script Magazine* (www.scriptmag.com)
- *Bang2Write* (www.bang2write.com)

Starting Small, Short and Simple

A big mistake that too many novices attempt is to "go big" and begin writing a Feature Film with no Outline, no proper Software, and no working knowledge of Structure, Character development, or even formatting.

My advice is this: start small, short and simple. Write a Short Film, no more than five pages and focus on no more than a couple of Characters. This will allow you to pay attention to the details without getting overwhelmed.

Figure out what Genre attracts your attention the most and download a few Feature Film Screenplays (in that Genre, preferably) to see what they look like. It used to be a task in itself to track down the precious official Screenplay of a Movie, and you often had to overpay for it. Now it is ridiculously simple and free (for most) to search for Screenplays within a database of thousands.

Once you download a PDF (the most common file format for a Script) and flip through it, you will get the idea even if you have never read one before. Make sure to search out Screenplays rather than Shooting Scripts for their readability (we will discuss the elements of a Shooting Script in Pre-Production). With the Screenplay, the biggest thing to pay attention is to the overall flow of it: how is the Dialogue formatted? How is the Action described? What goes in a Scene Heading? Then recreate that formatting to the best of your ability using whatever Word Processor (or even Typewriter) that you have access to.

Write a five-page (i.e., five minute) Script with Scene Headings, Action, Dialogue and maybe even a Transition or two. In the end, it won't really matter what you end up doing with it, because nobody is going to see this Script. Not this draft, and not at all until you learn more about Screenwriting, anyway.

Don't get me wrong, the premise might be brilliant, but I can guarantee that you didn't nail the details if you have never written a Script before. And rule #1 in Screenwriting is don't show it to somebody too early. In this case, if it's your first attempt at Screenwriting, you will not show it to anybody. But this is not an exercise in futility, I promise.

Now you will be doing it for real, and on a larger scale, if your ultimate goal is to create a Feature Film. You have gotten past the first hurdle of seeing what a Script really looks like, and re-creating that format has got to be the toughest part of Screenwriting, right?

Well, not exactly.

Suggested Software:

- Any Word Processor

Recommended Reading:

- *Writing Short Films* by Linda J. Cowgill

Online Resources:

- *Drew's Script-O-Rama* (www.script-o-rama.com)

Choosing a Concept

Choosing a Concept, the basic idea of what your Story is about, for your Feature Film is the single-most important decision that you can make regarding your Screenplay. Many select the first and perhaps only idea that happens to come into their mind without realizing what they are committing to. This is the biggest mistake of not only rookie Writers, but of those who fail to complete Scripts time and time again and usually end up giving up altogether.

This is why it is so important to spend the necessary time to select not only a marketable Concept but material that you really connect with. It will take time after you have trained your mind to think like a Writer, and it means paying attention to every passing thought to see if you may have a noteworthy idea for a Movie.

Speaking of "noteworthy," it is important to a Writer to have constant access to a note-taking system. It used to be the trusted pad of paper and pen in the pocket, but nowadays a more reasonable solution tends to be a phone app, preferably one that is tied in with a computer backup or cloud functionality, because it is almost always within reach when needed. I suggest both a written/typed system and a voice-recording setup to take advantage of times when it's easier to access one or the other. At a loud concert I'm more apt to use the typed version, and if I'm out and about I may resort to the voice recorder. Trust me, it's important to have both if you want to grab that idea immediately and hold on to it before it may be lost forever.

From there it is best to compile one document with all possible Script/Movie ideas. This way you can really see what you are working with when it comes to potential ideas, and choose the best project for you right now.

It may be that a certain Genre appeals to you, such as the same one in which you wrote your Short Film Script, or perhaps not. It may be that the idea dictates what type of Movie it will be. Whatever the case, it's important to identify a Concept that really stands out, because it leads directly into the next phase: Brainstorming.

Suggested Software:

- *Evernote* – syncs between phone/tablet/computer
- Any Voice Recorder phone app

Recommended Reading:

- *Made to Stick* by Chip Heath & Dan Heath
- *Screenwriting For Dummies* by Laura Schellhardt

Online Resources:
- *No Film School* (www.nofilmschool.com)
- *FAST Screenplay* (www.fastscreenplay.com)

Brainstorming

The very thought of Brainstorming may conjure up a bad taste in people's mouths because of past experiences in formal education. But if you have chosen a Genre that you enjoy watching Movies in (and you really should!) then certain aspects should come easy.

One good technique is to create a Mind Map with a circle in the middle. There are great apps and templates out there to help you with this. Then Brainstorm a Title and put it in the circle. Think of the catchy Titles of the Films in your Genre, and create something that identifies your Movie as such. Even if it's a working Title, stay away from something too vague, generic or boring. Now begin thinking of all the elements that could relate to this particular idea: Themes (i.e., what the Story is really about), Character traits, Plot Points, etc.

You will also use this Mind Map to determine what to pay particularly close attention to in the next phase: Research.

Suggested Software:
- *Idea Sketch* app

Recommended Reading:
- *Expect the Unexpected (Or You Won't Find it)* by Roger von Oech
- *Cracking Creativity: The Secrets of Creative Genius* by Michael Michalko

Online Resources:
- *Mind Tools* (www.mindtools.com)

Research

Now look up the most successful Movies in your chosen Genre (always study the best whenever possible!) and begin tracking down where you might find them.

It's neither recommended nor possible to watch every single Movie in a particular Genre: after all, you are doing this in order to write, eventually. But make sure that you identify and watch the key Films in your Concept's Genre. It is the worst thing to hear "your Script is great, but it's too much like (well-known Movie)" and the only thing you can claim from there is ignorance. Don't be that person, or you will get laughed out of the room.

This is my favorite part of the entire Writing process, and where I start to get really excited about the idea as the overall Concept begins to take shape. Plus, it's an excuse to tune out the world for a weekend and binge-watch whatever I can get my hands on that is in the selected Genre. Again this is why it's important to pick a Genre you enjoy, otherwise even this task could be painful.

I pay particular attention to what works and what doesn't in each Movie, what the Genre "rules" are (all Genres have them to a certain degree), and what the clichés are to make sure to avoid them and put a fresh spin on things. Beyond that, I just watch and enjoy, ready to pause and make notes at any given time and on any particular aspect that presents itself to me (Plot, Characters, overall tone, etc.).

During this phase I am also trying to track down any books, articles, Television shows, Documentaries, etc. about the subject matter that I am interested in covering, and I focus on taking lots of notes. It's prudent to find out what projects are currently in Development by reading the Trade Publications as well, to make sure there is nothing similar in Development that will be first to market. Always strive to be an expert on the subject you are writing about, even if it's more party conversation-level

8

than true expert panel. But hey, if you have the time to dive that deep, why not?

This process is all but guaranteed to make you a more interesting, knowledgeable person, so don't be afraid to learn things that you think you may not need for this particular Script. At this stage you really don't know what you will ultimately draw from.

The Research process may very well be an ongoing one all the way through Production, depending on the complexity of the subject matter and your own level of expertise in it. It's best to get a jump on it as soon as possible.

Suggested Software:
- *Wikipedia* app – use login to save searches
- *Can I Stream It?* app – locate Movies available online

Recommended Reading:
- *The Art of Watching Films* by Joseph M. Boggs and Dennis W. Petrie
- Anything relevant to your Concept and/or Genre

Online Resources:
- *Internet Movie Database* (www.imdb.com)
- *Rotten Tomatoes* (www.rottentomatoes.com)
- *Netflix* (www.netflix.com)
- *Variety* (www.variety.com)
- *Ain't It Cool News* (www.aintitcool.com)

Developing a Logline

Most of us are more familiar with Loglines than we even realize. Have you ever flipped through channels on your digital cable/satellite/streaming media box and noticed the short descriptions for programs? Those are essentially the

Loglines for those programs. And as you can now deduce, a Logline lives with a Movie for the entirety of its existence.

Loglines are simple yet complex at the same time, and must convey essential elements without trying to cram in too much. They are usually centered on the Main Character–possibly the Antagonist as well–and describe the main Conflict.

Crafting an intriguing Logline that flows well takes time and practice, but it's important to do it before you begin writing in order to keep your Story true to its original intent. It also becomes your most important Pitch tool throughout. Don't be afraid to try a few different Loglines and say them out loud to those closest to you. See what grabs their attention, what creates interest and what rolls off the tongue. This seemingly short and simple step can make all the difference in getting your project noticed when it comes time to market the Script.

You may very well end up revising it after completing your Screenplay, but get a Logline you feel solid about on paper before doing anything else, as it will keep your focus on track when writing the Three Paragraph Synopsis.

Suggested Software:
- Any Word Processor

Recommended Reading:
- *Loglines: The Long and Short on Writing Strong Loglines* by Douglas King

Online Resources:
- *The Internet Movie Logline Creator* (www.mitchmoldofsky.com/imlc.htm)
- *Script Anatomy* (www.scriptanatomy.com)

Writing the Three Paragraph Synopsis

The next logical step is one that I wasn't introduced to in my earlier years of Screenwriting, but wish I had been, and that is to sit down and write a simple Three Paragraph Synopsis. You only need three paragraphs: one for each Act, including a beginning, middle and end. Or an Introduction, Conflict, and Resolution, if you would like to view it that way, with the first two Acts culminating in major Plot Points.

The beauty of this step is that anybody can sit down and write three paragraphs, and do it in a single writing session. That is key in fact—to do it all at once. But don't worry, as this may never be seen externally, and you can always revise it later. So don't beat yourself up over the details since you only have a paragraph for each Act after all.

The Three Paragraph Synopsis is crucial for keeping you on track while Outlining, which is the next step.

Suggested Software:
- Any Word Processor

Recommended Reading:
- *Write a Great Synopsis–An Expert Guide* by Nicola Morgan

Online Resources:
- *Writer's Digest* (www.writersdigest.com)

Outlining

Most Screenwriters work backwards to some extent (i.e., they have a strong visual for an ending and craft a Story that ultimately leads them to that place). The beauty of Outlining is that it's a nonlinear process, so it's usually best to figure out where the major Scenes occur and basically connect the dots in-between.

A note about Story Structure here–there are several types of them (the traditional Three Act, the Hero's Journey, Save The Cat!, the Mini-Movie Method, etc.) which are too numerous and complex to get into in a book like this. Suffice it to say, it's crucial to pick the right match for your Story and Genre, and the Outlining stage is where it is easiest to shift these Scenes around to fit that Structure.

A tried-and-true method that some Writers still utilize is to Outline using 3x5 cards. Each Scene is summarized on a 3x5 card, which can then be placed or rearranged in any order necessary. There is also the popular Single Sheet Method (aka "Beat Sheet") to nail down the most critical Scenes.

A one or two sentence summary for each Scene should suffice if you are using one of the simpler methods at this stage. If you are using a Software program to Outline, they may prompt you to add in Character notes, etc. The more completely you fill these out, the easier the following steps will be.

While there are no rules about number of Scenes, most Feature Films fall within the range of 40-60 Scenes total. If you are in this range with your outlined Scenes, and feel like you have nailed all of your major Plot Points and can't seem to think of any other critical Scenes or Sequences–then it could be time to move on to the Treatment.

Suggested Software:

- *Movie Outline*
- *Storyist*

Recommended Reading:
- *Screenplay* by Syd Field
- *Save The Cat!* by Blake Snyder
- *Story* by Robert McKee
- *The Writer's Journey* by Christopher Vogler

Online Resources:
- *The Script Lab* (www.thescriptlab.com)

Writing the Treatment

Simply put, a Treatment is a description of the narrative Action that takes place in your Story. It is told in present tense, with each paragraph representing a new Scene and/or Sequence. To the untrained Writer this may appear to be a superfluous exercise. However, those that have used it as a tool understand its importance. It really helps to nail the narrative flow of your Story, so when it comes time to write the Screenplay, it will free you up to focus more on Character, Dialogue and other details.

Unlike the Outline and Three Paragraph Synopsis which are for your use only, the final Treatment will ultimately be a sales tool for your Screenplay. Desired lengths vary depending on its purpose and, frankly, who is asking for it, meaning that there really is no standardization. I have found in the past that a properly formatted Treatment that is not "overwritten" usually falls between seven and ten pages. If I'm in that range, I know that I'm doing alright for the amount of Story in my Screenplay.

There is a specific format and technique to writing a Treatment that is immediately apparent upon reading them. I have heard it called a book report for your Screenplay, and that's not too far off. Simplify the process by looking at a few sample Treatments before diving in.

Be sure to take some time after writing the initial draft of the Treatment to read it critically with an eye

13

toward revising it. Any Story Structure issues that are found and fixed at this stage will save a lot of headaches later, when writing the Screenplay.

Suggested Software:
* Any Word Processor

Recommended Reading:
* *Writing Treatments That Sell* by Kenneth Atchity and Chi-Li Wong

Online Resources:
* *The Writers Store* (www.writersstore.com)

Writing the Screenplay

The purpose of completing all the prior steps is to prepare you for writing the Screenplay. You may have been wondering why you can't just sit down and hash out a Feature Film Screenplay like you more or less did for the Short Film exercise. Simply put, it would be like trying to run in a marathon with no training regimen because you have been able to jog around the block. The Short Film Script and the Feature Film Screenplay are entirely different beasts, and it comes back to the preparation.

If you are serious about Screenwriting, I highly recommend investing in specialized Software. It not only keeps things formatted properly, but any of the good ones have a ton of shortcuts and other features as well. It is possible to type a Screenplay in a standard Word Processor if you set up custom tabs, etc. But for the rookie Writer especially, it is an extra step in the process to do so, and who needs that after all you have been through to get to this point. If you have the money, spend it (stated like a true Filmmaker, I know).

With the Treatment on the desk in front of you as your road map, take it Scene by Scene and slow and steady in writing the Screenplay. The nice part about this is the luxury of wandering without the risk of getting lost. You may find yourself literally copying and pasting some of the description from the Treatment into your Screenplay, and other times you may follow what a strong Character is telling you to say or do with them. There is no wrong way to go about it from here; just weave back to the next Scene in your Treatment, eventually.

It is of key importance as you are writing the first draft of your Screenplay to acknowledge up front that it will definitely need revising. Once you do this, it will free you up to charge forward without being overly critical of your writing. The urge to revise will come in, especially when feeling stuck at a part of your draft. Don't do it. Keep pressing forward until you have a complete draft before you even consider revising. There are too many stories out there of people trying to come out with the perfect first draft that end up never finishing it. Don't get bogged down with both sides of your brain battling it out. Let the creative juices flow, knowing that you can (and will!) revise when it's a finished draft. After all, you don't really know what you have until it's complete.

A Feature Film Screenplay should ultimately run between 90-120 pages. One minute of screen time equals one properly formatted Screenplay page. It's best to just aim for right around 100 pages to keep the math simple with Structure.

I don't mean to oversimplify, but just bang it out in a matter of a few weeks if possible. Then print it out and put it away in a drawer for about a month. Your subconscious mind will appreciate the break from writing, and the next time you will pick up the Screenplay will be with fresh eyes. Which is exactly what you will need for revising.

Suggested Software:
- *Final Draft*
- *Celtx*

Recommended Reading:
- *The Screenwriter's Bible* by David Trottier
- *The Complete Guide to Standard Script Formats–Part I: The Screenplay* by Cole and Haag
- *How to Write a Movie in 21 Days* by Viki King

Online Resources:
- *Keep Writing* (www.keepwriting.com)
- *ScreenwritingU* (www.screenwritingu.com)

Revising the Screenplay

The difference between a mediocre Writer and one that really shines is the developed skill of looking at your own work with objectivity. You had put away your Screenplay for a month, and by dusting it off you have hopefully detached yourself enough to look at it through fresh eyes.

So, what are you looking for? Everything... but not all at once. Give it an initial read-through (always try to read Screenplays in as few sittings as possible when revising) just to reacquaint yourself. It's amazing how much we can forget of our own work at this stage.

If you are one of those people that are annoyed by spelling, grammar and typos, then I suggest you begin by taking a red pen to your Screenplay and only look at those on the first pass. Keep in mind that if you make major changes to any Scene, getting micro on your syntax beforehand will be time wasted.

Then do another pass, looking only at the overall Structure of your Story. Then another critiquing only Character development. Then another for Action, Dialogue, description, formatting, etc. You get the idea:

with each pass look at only that aspect of it. It seems like a lot of work (and it is!) but it will be worth it to have a Script that is at least somewhat readable before sending it out for feedback.

Suggested Software:

- *ProWritingAid* – Plug-In for Word, Google Docs & Scrivener

Recommended Reading:

- *Your Screenplay Sucks!* by William M. Akers
- *Making a Good Script Great* by Linda Seger

Online Resources:

- *MasterWriter* (www.masterwriter.com)

Getting Feedback on the Screenplay

At this point, it is wise to either register your Screenplay with the Writers Guild of America (WGA) and/or the US Copyright Office because you will be sending it out to be read by a perfect stranger. This is a relatively simple and inexpensive online process. Registering your Screenplay will protect your material so that you can feel confident showing it to anybody moving forward.

Script-reading services abound on the internet these days. I will say that most are reputable, but I do advise checking out their online reviews before committing to one. Getting truly professional Script Coverage is critical, especially for a rookie Screenwriter. A professional Script-reading is not necessarily cheap, but in the grand scheme of Filmmaking, this really is a crucial step that will pay dividends well beyond in the knowledge you will acquire from the feedback.

What you thought was a polished Screenplay may not be in the eyes of somebody that reads them every day. Their responses may even seem a bit jaded if they can sniff out a novice, but it will be some of the most helpful feedback you will get. Plus I've always felt that it's better to get critical feedback at the Screenplay stage than it is to get a scathing review of the finished Movie when it's too late to make changes.

Still, even if you pay for a professional reader, it is only one opinion. You may want to consider sending copies to a few close friends and family members–preferably Movie buffs–that have an understanding of Movies in the Genre you have written in. Try to send them digital copies, as PDFs are great and read well on most tablets. If they're not into that, then you may have to plan on printing up a few copies. Luckily most professionals these days actually prefer PDF format, so that cuts down on cost and materials considerably.

After gathering up both the professional and amateur (yet trusted) feedback, compile their notes and decide which changes you are going to commit to making. You will be sick of your Script by this point, and probably ready to give up on the whole process after likely getting a "Pass" (overall negative review) on the professional Script Coverage. Just try to focus on the positive, making sure not to tinker with what works and trying to fix what doesn't. Also know that this relatively little amount of work in the grand scheme of the Filmmaking process as a whole could make all the difference between a hit Movie and a total flop.

You'll soon find out what difference it made if you enter it in any Script Contests and Pitch Fests.

Suggested Software:
- *Final Draft* – direct link to WGA registration
- *Movie Outline* – direct link to registering/reading services

Online Resources:

- *Writers Guild of America* (www.wga.org)
- *US Copyright Office* (www.copyright.gov)
- *Hollywood Script Express*
  (www.hollywoodscriptexpress.com)
- *Script Pipeline* (www.scriptpipeline.com)
- *Coverage, Ink* (www.coverageink.com)

Script Contests and Pitch Fests

Though this book is geared toward the Filmmaker who is intending to produce their Movie independently, Script Contests and Pitch Fests have a place in the process.

I see them as a worthwhile option as you move into the Financing and/or Pre-Production stage. This is an opportunity to get your project some notoriety as a Contest winner and/or finalist, and it's good practical experience. Pitching is an essential part of the business and more or less how the business works at the highest levels. You will hopefully get some more constructive feedback both on your Script and on how you plan on marketing your eventual Movie. Again, there are many Script Contests and Pitch Fests, so research the ones that seem worthwhile and are a good fit for your Screenplay.

There is also a formality to the way things are done, so be prepared to have what amounts to a Query Letter. A Query Letter should include your Logline and a bit about yourself and is basically your written Pitch for most Script Contests and Pitch Fests.

Pitching is an art in and of itself, and learning the accepted format of a Pitch meeting is crucial in separating yourself from the pack. So much of this business is about perception; if you can come off as a professional that is familiar with and respectful of the way that things are done, you should get the opportunity for your ideas to be heard.

You will be notified in advance how much time you

are given with any potential Buyer/Investor at a Pitch Fest. It is important for your Pitch to sound sharp without being too rehearsed. The most common format is the 60-second Pitch, but it's good to practice longer and shorter variations as well.

The more feedback that you get in these settings, the more you will be able to see where your Screenplay (and finished Movie) fits into the marketplace. You will also get an idea of a realistic Budget level to expect, and which avenue to pursue from here: Self-Financing, private Investors or Studios.

Recommended Reading:
- *Selling Your Story in 60 Seconds* by Michael Hauge
- *Good in a Room* by Stephanie Palmer
- *33 Ways to Sell Your Screenplay* by Hal Croasmun

Online Resources:
- *International Screenwriters Association* (www.networkisa.org)
- *Stage 32* (www.stage32.com)
- *ScreenCraft* (www.screencraft.org)

PART 2
PRE-PRODUCTION SIMPLIFIED

Making your First Film

If you have never made a Film before, you really need to complete the process all the way through on a micro scale before you can tackle the longer and more complex material of a Feature Film.

My suggestion is to follow your pets around with a Camera. Seriously! If you don't have any pets, then try to film wildlife. If you can't find any wildlife, then just shoot landscape/still life Shots that tell some sort of visual Story. Try to borrow or rent a real Camera (not a phone) so you can get the additional experience of working with them. Read the Camera manual and/or watch instructional Videos online to get a firm grasp of its basic operation. Experiment with different settings.

Don't waste anybody else's time by asking them to help as you fumble your way through making your first Film. You will need their help and cooperation later, and you probably don't want any witnesses to your embarrassing first effort at Directing.

Take the Footage you have shot and start Editing it. There is an abundance of inexpensive Editing Software out there for sale, as well as cloud options and/or full purchase Software options available for immediate download. Add Music (any will work for now since you won't be screening this anywhere), Titles, and Transitions (but not too many).

Most importantly, just finish it! Become a Filmmaker the only way possible–by making a Film.

Only show the finished product to your closest circle of friends, even if you think it's good, and get some honest feedback. Make the changes for the exercise in applying feedback and in keeping your friends on your side by showing that you care enough about your art to listen to their input. This is how you butter them up for the inevitable favors you will be asking of them when making your Feature Film.

Note what was difficult about the process and where you felt uncomfortable. Those are your weaknesses, and where you will inevitably need the most help down the road. This is what you will hire out for whenever possible as opposed to which duties you will want to take on yourself.

Recommended Reading:
- *Making a Winning Short* by Edmond Levy
- *Filmmaking For Dummies* by Bryan Michael Stoller

Online Resources:
- *Videomaker Magazine* (www.videomaker.com)
- *MasterClass* (www.masterclass.com) – tutorials

Forming a Production Company

There are two basic approaches to creating a company: you can form a general Production Company that will be your umbrella for all of your projects moving forward (recommended if you're more of a lone wolf or have a tight-knit team), or you can form one that exists solely for the current Film project (better if you are going in on this with people you are otherwise unfamiliar in working with).

There are several ways to go about forming your Company beyond this, and the rules vary between states and countries. The costs of starting your company will be another investment that will have to be fronted, so make sure to choose the type (sole proprietorship, LLC, etc.) wisely.

Keeping it simple is the best approach here, and online resources abound in order to save on extraneous legal fees. You will need to legally form a Production Company for various aspects of the Production itself

(Permits, Insurance, etc.) or to even get in a room with potential Investors during the next phase of Fundraising and Financing.

Recommended Reading:
- *The Beginning Filmmaker's Business Guide* by Renee Harmon

Online Resources:
- *LegalZoom* (www.legalzoom.com)

Fundraising & Financing

If you are fortunate enough to be in a position to finance your own Film, this section is more or less irrelevant to you. Then again, why spend your own money making Films when you could find somebody else to foot the bill? For a share in the profits, of course.

However, this seems to be the question that most everybody has: where does the money come from? The truth is that there is no real stock answer here, as it depends on who you are, what type of Film you are making, and sometimes, just plain dumb luck.

Are you making something in the documentary / educational realm or does it address a specific issue? Maybe a grant would be enough to get you going. Is your Story a commercially viable High Concept Script? A Film Market might be the place to get it pre-sold. Do you have a rich uncle that adores you? Hit him up for the cash. Just know that if you don't return on the investment, he may not speak to you again. Is it worth the risk? That's for you to decide.

Crowdfunding is a tempting option, but know that it seems to be a struggle for unknown artists to finance this way (especially enough for a Feature Film). Crowdfunding seems more geared toward established presences and/or must-have tech products.

The most common types of Investors in independent Film seem to be groups of Angel Investors that are typically searching for specific Genres–and oftentimes a full slate–of Movies. It will be an uphill battle to convince anybody that you're worth the risk as a first time Filmmaker. But if you know how to approach it the right way (i.e., know how the game is played), it will be to your advantage, and you may just find the right fit to get your Movie made.

Recommended Reading:
- *Filmmakers and Financing: Business Plans for Independents* by Louise Levison

Online Resources:
- *IndieWire* (www.indiewire.com)

Hiring Production Staff

Hiring a hard-working, experienced and reliable Production Staff is of the utmost importance, as all technical (and several creative) aspects of your Film will rely upon their competence and will be enhanced by their skills. The key is to hire a handful of Department Heads and trust that they will bring the best and brightest from their own networks to work under them when it's time to begin Production.

While this has proven to be an effective strategy time and time again, people outside of the business claim that it is driven by nepotism. The truth is that you will be spending 10-14 hours a day with this group, so why not spend it with people that are friendly, trustworthy (and of course brilliant at their Crew position as well)?

The Line Producer is responsible for preparing the Budget and seeing that the Production doesn't go over its projections. In Pre-Production this means a lot of adjustment of the Budget, as the projected numbers become reality and as each line item is secured for the Production. This needs to be somebody with direct experience as they will be a problem solver on Budget issues throughout the Filmmaking process.

The Production Manager will assist the Line Producer with finalizing the Budget as well as scheduling. A good Production Manager will maximize your shoot days. It is through their expertise that it will become clear where your biggest challenges lie in bringing your (hopefully ambitious) project to life. Experience matters here; don't hire a friend to "figure it out as you go," as this will inevitably lead to a perilous outcome for the project or friendship, or both.

The First Assistant Director (AD) will help with the final tweaking of schedules, making sure that overtimes, turnarounds and breaks are accounted for. They will also help run your Set and are a crucial part in maintaining the efficiency of the Shoot. Again, experience and character matters here, as the AD will be the go-between for almost all Crew departments, Cast members and Extras on Set. It is a stressful job and it's important not to have a short temper. Usually they know some good Second ADs that can help out for certain days on larger Sets by wrangling Extras, Staging crowd Scenes, etc.

The Director of Photography (DP) is ultimately responsible for the overall look of the Film and will help give a rookie Director some much needed tips on Continuity. Because the DP is such a crucial part of the team, their experience, which is usually judged by the quality of their Reel of work, is key. A good DP will usually know a top-notch Gaffer who will know some Grips and Electrics, and so on. If you're really lucky, they may even have the latest and greatest Camera, or at least know where to get a solid deal from a Rental House.

A Production Accountant will be necessary as well, to make sure that your Budget stays on track and all money is, well... accounted for. If you have somebody in your network with accounting experience, this could be a position for them, but a working vocabulary of the Movie business is helpful, too.

Your Film may need roles filled well in advance, including a Production Designer, Art Director, Set Builders, Special Effects Supervisor, etc., depending on the specific needs of the Production. Again, it's all about lead times and synchronizing everything to be ready on the day it is needed for the Shoot.

I know there are some mavericks out there that are going to attempt to do it all themselves; more power to you if you can pull it off. But the entire process will be more enjoyable if you can at least hire these key positions while still in Pre-Production. Because once you start shooting, it's all too easy for certain things to get derailed if you don't have somebody looking after these aspects full-time.

Recommended Reading:
- *What a Producer Does* by Buck Houghton

Online Resources:
- *Mandy Film & TV Production Resources* (www.mandy.com)
- *ProductionHUB* (www.productionhub.com)

Script Breakdown

This is when you should begin turning the Screenplay into a Shooting Script—which includes Scene Numbers, Revision Marks and is divided into specific Shots. The updated Shooting Script will be an ongoing process throughout the shoot, with last-minute Revisions a common scenario.

The execution of the Script Breakdown is primarily the responsibility of the Assistant Director (AD). They break down each Scene or Sequence to the various

Production aspects: Cast, Location, Props, FX, Sound, etc.

What used to be accomplished using a complex system of printed strips and a large Production Board is now done through Software programs that take all considerations into account and figure out what takes priority in every Scene. The AD estimates the number of shoot days, which is a key factor.

Once you have a Script Breakdown that makes sense and is agreed upon by everyone, the Line Producer has the information they need and will draw up a Budget.

Suggested Software:
- *Movie Magic Scheduling*
- *Final Draft Tagger*

Recommended Reading:
- *Film Scheduling* by Ralph S. Singleton

Online Resources:
- *FilmSkills* (www.filmskills.com)
- *HowToFilmSchool* (www.howtofilmschool.com)

Budgeting

Budgeting is a necessary evil, and a Film Budget is done differently than, say, a household Budget. Yet the same principles hold true. Creating a Budget is the key responsibility of the Line Producer, but it is up to the entire Producing team to have a working understanding of at least the Top Sheet of the Budget.

The Top Sheet is a breakdown of the Budget which represents the totals allotted for each department. Working backwards, you know that you have a certain amount of money to spend in total: from Pre-Production to the Distribution of the Film (whatever you raised with the Investors and/or Self-Financed), and now it is time to allocate those funds to the appropriate departments based on the Script Breakdown.

Department Heads will always fight for more money for their aspect of the Production, but it is up to the Line Producer, Production Manager and Executive Producer (if applicable) to make the final decision. It is also important to factor in a percentage of total Budget (usually 10%) as an Overage. This is basically a monetary cushion in case one or more of the departments go over Budget, and it happens more than the Movie industry likes to admit.

There are plenty of Budget templates out there, and a good starting point is the SAG (Screen Actors Guild) Low and Ultra Low-Budget Agreements. There are also good Software programs out there created specifically for Film Budgets, or just a plain old spreadsheet will do. It's really about the level of trust placed in the numbers to match your Production, and that can only come with experience.

If your Budget is on a shoestring and you can't for whatever reason afford to hire a Line Producer, at least consider consulting with one over the Budget and have them give some feedback before proceeding on to Casting.

Suggested Software:
- *Movie Magic Budgeting*
- *Gorilla Budgeting*

Recommended Reading:
- *Film + Video Budgets* by Deke Simon
- IFP *West Independent Filmmaker's Manual* by Nicole Shay LaLoggia & Eden H. Wurmfeld

Online Resources:
- *SAG-AFTRA Labor Union* (www.sagaftra.org)
- *IATSE Labor Union* (www.iatse.net)
- *Quick Film Budget* (www.quickfilmbudget.com)

Casting

The logistics of the Production are finally taking shape, you have an idea of the number of shoot dates for each Role, and you know when you would ideally film these Scenes. If you choose to forego hiring a Casting Director—who can be very useful for their knowledge, insight and contacts—then the primary responsibility of Casting will fall on the Producer(s) and Director.

Auditioning for Movies seems to be going the way of the dinosaur these days, and for good reason. Any serious Actor has a Reel or at least a link to several of their finished works online. Don't waste their time and yours by having them Audition, as many Actors are willing to travel great distances to come work on a Film but perhaps not to "just" an Audition. It's usually a monetary choice for them at that point, as they aren't getting paid to Audition.

Advertise on whatever local Acting sites you can find, and post flyers at any artistic hubs in your city. Have Actors email you the appropriate résumé and contact information (including their Headshot and Reel) and be sure to look at (not necessarily respond to) each one. If they don't have any examples near the Character you are looking for, send them a follow-up asking for any other work in the same Genre as your Film.

If you have an aspiring Actor that has only done Modeling or other forms of on-screen Talent work (i.e., doesn't have any sort of Reel to show) and it's a major Role in the Film, then it would be worth considering an informal video chat and Script-reading (not a formal Audition) to determine if they have what it takes for the Role.

Once you have narrowed your prospects, email them the Script, letting them know which part you would like them to play. If you don't hear back from them, either they didn't like the Role or the Script as a whole, or they are flaky and you should move on from dealing with them. If they follow up and seem enthusiastic, this could be your target.

At this point it's worth having a phone or video chat just to make sure they are on the same page creatively and logistically. From there you should have the information you need to make your decision and make them an offer.

Suggested Software:

- *Skype* app

Recommended Reading:

- *Casting Revealed: A Guide for Film Directors* by Hester Schell

Online Resources:

- *Backstage* (www.backstage.com)
- *Craigslist* (www.craigslist.org)

Contracts & Releases

Ahhh... glorious paperwork! That's why we all got into this business after all, right? I'm joking, but it's important to get all of this squared away, and the earlier the better.

If you are dealing with big time Actors, Contracts will be handled through their Agents, but the burden of the initial preparation will still fall to your team. Don't worry, though, as there are lots of boilerplate Contracts out there that are good starting points. If you are dealing directly with the Actors it can be simpler, but it's important to be clear upon signing about what is expected of them so there are no disputes later. Too many horror stories exist due to contractual misunderstandings and Actors overbooking, leaving Productions in limbo unless or until that Actor can return.

Crew members usually sign a Deal Memo which lays out the start date, how many days of work are expected on the Production, the Day Rate and any other considerations. If they are Below-The-Line (Grips, Gaffers, etc.) this is pretty standard practice. Above-The-Line (Producers, Director, DP) usually have more considerations involved, such as Back-End Pay or Royalties, and therefore sign a Contract instead.

Image Release Forms are important to get signed from anybody appearing on-screen. Releases are also necessary if any Artwork, Stock Footage, Clips from Broadcasts or other Movies, Sound Bites, Photographs, etc. appear in your Final Edit, so it's important to consider that while planning the Shoot.

These items can and will be asked for by Festivals and Television Networks planning on airing your finished Movie, so keep them on file and be prepared to show them down the road. Unlike a reality TV program, blurring somebody's face can be very distracting in a Movie and really take the viewer out of the experience. More than that, it just rings of an amateur that didn't have their paperwork together. As a double whammy, it will cost you to blur faces and/or attempt to remove them in Post-Production.

Suggested Software:

- *Litwak's Multimedia Producer's Handbook* (CD-ROM)

Recommended Reading:

- *Contracts for the Film & Television Industry* by Mark Litwak
- *The Pocket Lawyer for Filmmakers* by Thomas A. Crowell, Esq.

Online Resources:

- *Film Contracts* (www.filmcontracts.net)
- *Independent Filmmaker Contracts* (www.independentfilmmakercontracts.com)
- *Film Crew Builder* (www.filmcrewbuilder.com)

Location Scouting & Permits

If you have several Locations to deal with on your Script Breakdown, then Location Scouting could become a full-time job (quite literally). This is where it might be wise to hire a Location Manager. They work closely with the Production Manager in finding the perfect settings for your Script based on a variety of factors.

The first is, of course, how closely does it portray what is being described? Next is, how realistic would it be to shoot there logistically? Is it hundreds of miles from the Production office? Does it have facilities such as parking for Production trucks, bathrooms and/or civilization in general nearby? Is the owner charging an arm and a leg for use of the Location? Is it near a highway or airport where Sound will be an issue? These are all considerations to weigh.

Once the preliminary targets are narrowed down by the Location Manager (and/or Production Manager) and after furthering narrowing by doing a preliminary search online (using Google Earth or a similar site), it is wise to get out to as many sites as you can as Director. And bring your DP with you as they are sure to have some feedback as well.

Also worth mentioning here is taking a look at any Sound Stages that may be in the area. They could be a good fallback option for shooting some hard to find Interior or Green Screen Scenes if it makes budgetary sense. Keep in mind that you will need to construct Sets if shooting at a Sound Stage, but they may have helpful resources or amenities to help offset those costs.

If the Location is private property, it may be difficult to track down the property owner and convince them to let you shoot there. Be sure to approach Location owners with their needs in mind. If it's a business, what hours are they closed and is it feasible to shoot then? Are they willing to negotiate a price that makes them cooperative? Offer them Special Thanks; make reassurances that your Crew will leave as small a footprint as possible and have integrity in keeping your word. Plus, you never know when you may need to go back for Pick-ups or Reshoots.

If it is public (i.e., government) land, then the real catch is figuring out what kind of Permits might be necessary. Permits are usually not altogether that expensive, but there is bureaucracy involved. The agency granting the Permit will want to see the Script and get it approved by the local Film Commissioner, which can be a nightmare in and of itself. They will definitely ask to see the Certificate of Insurance (COI) before approving anything as well. On the bright side, the Film Office can be a big help in tracking down other resources or supplying a local Production Directory—most states and/or metro areas have them now—filled with local companies and organizations.

There are definitely ways around Permits in certain instances–especially in more rural areas where Film Productions don't make up a measurable part of the economy–but it's at the risk of shutting down the Shoot for the day. I only recommend going without if you are not trespassing or doing anything dangerous, if you are not planting a Camera down on the ground (i.e., using a handheld rig not on Tripod), and you are only shooting with one or two Actors and a skeleton Crew.

If you have a large Scene with lots of people involved, it's best to play by the rules, as you will have a lot less stress in the end. Don't even think about shooting Guerilla style if you are doing Stunts, shutting down streets, or have any sort of fire or explosions.

You are risking a criminal record and lawsuits at that point, and no Movie is worth that.

Suggested Software:
- *MapAPic Location Scout* app
- *Panascout* app

Recommended Reading:
- *Shoot on Location* by Kathy M. McCurdy

Online Resources:
- *Google Earth* (www.google.com/earth)

Refining the Schedule

Now that everybody is on board, Locations are scouted and you have a start date for the Production, it's time to refine the Schedule. The biggest aspect of this is assigning specific dates to Scenes, now that you have the information you need to make these decisions.

Did your Lead Actor book an Audition on a day you had originally scheduled to be their big solo Scene? Did a major Location specify dates of availability that differ from what you had laid out?

Then it's back to the drawing board, more or less. Hopefully less. As in, try to bump things as little as possible and keep it simple. Better yet, let your Production Manager worry about it; just know what they are going through and don't be ignorant to the process.

A six-day work week is industry standard, with ten-hour days for Cast and Crew typical. Overtime is an unavoidable reality and should be budgeted in, but keeping your Crew on schedule as much as possible will keep their morale up. Production is a tough grind, but an experienced Crew will know what they are in for and how to pace themselves.

A big morale killer is a Short Turnaround. The Unions fight this aspect of Production tooth and nail, as it really is unhealthy for people to work late into the night only to have a sunrise Call Time the next day. A good Assistant Director will be keenly aware of this, but you should be, too. You want people to come work for you on your next Film, and you don't want them to tell their network how you overworked them.

Suggested Software:
- *Movie Magic Scheduling*

Recommended Reading:
- *Before You Shoot* by Helen Garvy

Production Insurance

Production Insurance is another of those necessary evils that needs to be discussed when doing anything even remotely dangerous involving either people or equipment. One way around it on a safe, mellow Set is to use your own Gear and have your Talent and Crew sign a Liability Waiver. But if you are asking them to do something dangerous, then you should really ante up for Production Insurance.

If you rent your Production Gear, most likely they will ask for a Certificate of Insurance. If you bought your equipment, most likely you will want it to cover your own. If you are a homeowner (or renter) with Insurance it is possible that you can be covered through that policy, but usually with the limitation that you are only filming on your own property. It's always best to find out what exactly is covered on your current policy and go from there.

You will need to purchase Insurance for all Production dates and to specify a total amount (based on how much everything is worth), what kind of stuff you are filming (Stunts, Explosions, etc. add liability), and where you are shooting (Location can make a difference as to premiums as well). There are lots of choices available online, and most standard Insurance companies can at least refer you to one if not provide a form of the coverage themselves.

Don't take any chances in this area; it's not worth your financial future and not worth the added stress of trying to do something Guerilla style (without Permits or Insurance) rather than legally.

Recommended Reading:
- *Production Management for TV and Film* by Linda Stradling

Online Resources:
- *Movie Insure* (www.movieinsure.com)
- *Production Insurance* (www.productioninsurance.com)

Early Rehearsal

Rehearsing with Actors well in advance of a Shoot is a nice luxury to have that realistically doesn't happen all that often on low-budget Productions.

You'll be lucky to even get a Table Read out of everybody, where all or most of the Actors sit down and read the Script through with the Writer and/or Director reading the Action in the Script. Table Reads on a low-budget Film seem to be rare nowadays, as people's schedules are only more and more complicated to sort out. If you do get an opportunity where this seems feasible, by all means attempt to organize one. Just getting your Actors to read the Script through in front of you is a great way to see how close they are to nailing the Characters, if they have any questions about the Story, or if the Script reads poorly in any areas (especially Dialogue).

If you do get time to Rehearse your Actors in advance, work on the overall Staging of Scenes. Get as much of the Staging down as you can, without getting too micro—as it will inevitably change a bit On-Set dependent on the Location and other variables. Having a rough idea will help with your Shot List & Storyboards.

Recommended Reading:
- *Directing Actors* by Judith Weston
- *Film Directing: Cinematic Motion* by Steven D. Katz

Online Resources:
- *Mastering Film* (www.masteringfilm.com)

Shot List & Storyboards

Creating a Shot List and/or Storyboards is a crucial part of the visualization process for a Director. It really is Directing on paper, at least as far as Shot selection is concerned.

As somebody that cannot draw to save my life, I had resorted for years to using a Shot List. A Shot List is simply a grid made up with Scene & Shot number, Shot size (Close-Up, Medium, Wide, etc.), Movement (Dolly, Handheld, etc.), whether it is an Interior (INT.) or Exterior (EXT.) shot, Time of Day, Shot Description, and any special Notes (usually things to look out for when setting up the Shot). While this is a great solution for a simple Production without too many variables, it can be limiting for those doing larger, more complex Scenes, as a Shot List will most likely require other departments' input to have the Director's vision clear in their minds.

This is really where Storyboarding comes into play. Storyboarding visually communicates what a Shot List can only attempt to do with words. And as the saying goes, a picture is worth a thousand words. What used to be prohibitive about Storyboarding was either needing to have talent in drawing, or having to factor in the cost of hiring a Storyboard Artist.

Nowadays, however, there are great Software options that allow you to combine their stock Characters and images with Location Scouting Photos (for backgrounds) and elements downloaded off the web. You no longer need to be a sketch artist to communicate the visual representation of the Shot, which is really the whole purpose of a Storyboard. These Software solutions can really save a lot of time and embarrassment (if you draw like I do!).

If you really want to take your Directing capabilities to another level, the process of Pre-Visualization can take your Storyboard art and add motion and timing to it. This is a useful tool for communicating lots of specific information to different departments and also for deepening your understanding of the relationship of Shots (i.e., how it will all cut together in Editing).

Suggested Software:
- *Storyboard Quick*
- *FrameForge Previz Studio*

Recommended Reading:
- *Storyboarding 101* by James O. Fraioli
- *Cinematic Storytelling* by Jennifer Van Sijll

Online Resources:
- *Storyboard That* (www.storyboardthat.com)

Gear Rentals

Now that you have the Film scheduled and Pre-Visualized through the Shot List and Storyboards, you will know what Production Gear it's going to take to accomplish your vision. You also have Production Insurance which will come in crucial at this step, as any legitimate Rental house will ask to see your COI and/or provide you with their own (if you are lucky). Although the Rental house will usually only provide Insurance for an added charge, and it will only cover their Gear.

For a novice Director, trusting your DP and Gaffer to make a wish list will be really helpful. On bigger Productions it's standard to hire Grip Trucks that come packed with Gear, whereas on smaller ones you can pick and choose your Rentals. But you must create a comprehensive Gear List either way. It's important to walk the line of staying within Budget versus keeping your Camera Crew happy with the tools they have to work with.

It will all seem like a lot of Gear (and most likely money) is needed. But when all is said and done, if you have the right tools and the right people operating them, your Film will have what is usually referred to as Production Value. Making sure to book all of this well in advance is crucial to getting the right equipment for the right price. It's obvious that there's no Production without a Camera, and it's a huge consideration as to which type, but there are so many other factors to weigh here as well.

Most of the time you can get a weekly deal such as only being charged for three days of a week, or if you are shooting weekends, you can get deals for that as well. A lot of Gear Rental houses will work with you on price, especially if you get all of your stuff from the same facility. Finding certain specialized Equipment used to require living near and/or driving to a metropolitan area, but nowadays there are lots of online Rental sites that factor in the shipping costs, enabling you to get what you need no matter where you live or plan to shoot.

It's important to stage your Production Gear when checking out, which includes making sure that everything is there and works properly, and allotting an appropriate amount of time for this process. The worst thing is to get out on Set only to discover a certain accessory is missing a part, rendering the Camera or other crucial component inoperable. This can hold up or even shut down a Production for the day, so don't ignore this step!

Recommended Reading:
- *The Grip Book* by Michael G. Uva
- *Set Lighting Technician's Handbook* by Harry C. Box

Online Resources:
- *ProGear Rental* (www.progearrental.com)
- *BorrowLenses* (www.borrowlenses.com)

Props, Costumes & Wardrobe

This is an ideal phase to focus on gathering Props, scheduling fittings for Costumes, and figuring out Wardrobe accessories for at least the first several Scenes that you will be shooting (if not the whole Film). Getting a jump on these things will inevitably save you headaches, where procrastinating may force you to make some decisions that will sacrifice the look of the overall Movie.

On a historical or sci-fi Film (or any crowd Scenes) it may be necessary to have a large department for each of these aspects. On a small Production, you may have a Prop Master and another person handling Costume and Wardrobe. It is very helpful to have these positions on Set as the Director has enough to worry about. And having somebody focused entirely on these details will help everything run more smoothly.

If you are attempting to handle Props, Costumes and Wardrobe yourself and/or you are on a tight Budget, flea markets and thrift stores are a great resource. Always start at the cheapest places hoping to get lucky, and work your way up to full-on Costume Rental shops if need be. Another place to try is a local Theatre Company, as they may have what you're looking for and could be looking to make a few bucks on the side. It's always good to take along somebody that has an eye for this stuff so you can discuss whether it fits the Scene, Character or Movie as a whole.

Recommended Reading:
- *The Prop Building Guidebook* by Eric Hart
- *Costuming for Film* by Holly Cole and Kristin Burke

Online Resources:
- *Independent Studio Services* (www.issprops.com)
- *Western Costume Company* (www.westerncostume.com)

Catering & Craft Services

Catering (i.e., meals) should be arranged well in advance of the Shoot, and ideally you would have the same company on board for every major Production day. This is the most economical way to feed your Cast and Crew, saving you from having to make trips for pizza or sandwiches every day (which is especially time-consuming if you are shooting remotely). The best Catering companies are in high demand for all sorts of special events, so contacting them as soon as you have Shoot dates set and the wheels in motion is advisable.

A great Catering company will understand the need for a healthy, tasty variety of food and should be able to prepare it for serving on Location and be able to accommodate any and all special dietary needs (gluten-free, allergies, vegetarian, etc.). That kind of concern can go a long way and help all parties feel included, and it really does build the communal aspects of making a project together. For those lacking in choice of Catering companies due to geography, any food truck should do the trick so long as they fit the above requirements.

Craft Services (i.e., snacks and beverages) should be present and on-hand throughout the day, within a short distance from the Set. Again, a healthy assortment of snacks such as trail mix and granola bars is preferable to anything too sugary or heavy. Coffee and caffeine are a must, as people will need it to keep going throughout a long Production day. Somebody–usually a Production Assistant (PA) on small Sets but it could be a dedicated Craft Services person–needs to keep this station clean and re-stocked at all times as well. If you're doing your own shopping here, a big box store will be a great resource for bulk goods.

The bottom line is, don't skimp on food and snacks if you want a happy Crew. I have worked on Sets where people were getting low-to-no pay but being fed well, and I have worked on Sets where people were making solid money but the eats were subpar. I'll let you guess which ones had the better morale. A well-fed Crew is a happy Crew!

Recommended Reading:

- *Secrets from a Caterer's Kitchen* by Nicole Aloni

Online Resources:

- *Gigante Catering* (www.gigantecatering.com)

PART 3
PRODUCTION SIMPLIFIED

Learning the Language

So the big day has finally come; the first day of the Shoot (aka Principal Photography). Like any workplace, a Movie Set has its own Language and slang. It is important for the novice Director to pick up on the meaning of some of these terms immediately, while developing rapport with the Crew. The best way to accomplish this is incidentally the best way to learn, and that is to not be afraid to ask questions.

Filmmaking is such a specialized craft that it is alright for the Director to not understand all the uses for a C-Stand or Gaffer Tape (seemingly endless, by the way) but rather to have an understanding that asking for certain things will take time and effort by somebody on the Crew. Score some bonus points by learning the "Over/Under Technique" of properly coiling cable if you don't know already. Those little things go a long way toward subtly showing that you aren't useless as a Crew hand.

The energy that you bring to the Set will be the energy that your Crew gives back tenfold. That can work adversely too, so just like any leadership position, it comes with a certain level of responsibility. Don't show up unprepared, hungover, or distracted by personal issues. It's the least you can do to try to be liked by the Crew. You will be spending lots of long days together in rather uncomfortable situations at times. At least show some genuine interest in their part of the collaborative process.

The smaller the Crew is, the more that you will have to get hands-on with these positions. Always offer and be ready to help strike at least some small items on Set. Don't have an ego over this kind of situation, and save it for when it really counts. You will need to have a bit of a creative ego (or downright stubbornness) in order to press forward and get what you need while inevitably making concessions along the way, trust me.

Recommended Reading:
- *The Beginning Filmmaker's Guide to Directing* by Renee Harmon
- *Feature Filmmaking at Used-Car Prices* by Rick Schmidt

Online Resources:
- *FilmLand* (www.filmland.com/glossary/Dictionary.html)
- *The Anonymous Production Assistant* (www.anonymousproductionassistant.com)
- *The Black and Blue* (www.theblackandblue.com)

On-Set Rehearsal

If you had a chance to do a Table Read and/or Rehearsal with your Actors in Pre-Production, then you're ahead of the game. If not, don't worry; it just means you will probably be spending more time (and Takes) explaining Character motivations during On-Set Rehearsal.

I always try to greet Actors upon their arrival and make sure they understand what the plan is for the day. This is important so that they can get their subconscious geared up for certain Scenes, ultimately leading to better performances. If you have any last-minute Script changes, be sure to hand them over before the Actor gets into Hair & Makeup, which can be a perfect place for them to have time to review the changes.

It's generally understood that if you're working with a Star—most likely as a "Day Player" on your early Movies—they will demand more attention, but this isn't always the case. It's important to make sure that their needs are taken care of (you will hear from an Assistant of theirs if not!). But it's also important to maintain balance on your Set, as your energy is sure to be pulled a thousand different ways with questions and such.

The key to Rehearsing Actors on Set is to find that happy medium where they are nailing their Dialogue and Blocking in the Run-Through, but saving their best performances for the Camera. Some Actors need very little Rehearsal while others seem to need a lot. You will know from the first couple of Takes, and you can always Rehearse a bit more in-between Takes as well. Don't be rigid to suggestion at this stage, as this is where some of the best Improvisation can come from. But know what you need to get emotionally out of every Scene and Shot.

If an Actor just isn't getting across what you need for the Scene, sometimes telling them to play it totally opposite for a Take loosens them up a bit. It's important to get what you know you need but also leave some room and time for Improvisation. Usually I allow this on a Safety Take (after you know you have gotten at least one solid Take filmed already), and often it turns out to be their best stuff because the pressure is off.

I live by the rule that I would never ask an Actor to do something that I wouldn't do myself, a sort of Director's version of the Golden Rule. I also practice positive reinforcement only, never saying "no, that wasn't it," but rather, "that was good, let's try another take just to make sure we have it." This has turned out to be a positive way to maintain trust with Actors, giving them confidence in your judgment and building more confidence in themselves. This inevitably leads to greater efforts all around and a Film with better performances.

Recommended Reading:
- *Changing Direction* by Lenore DeKoven
- *Acting for the Camera* by Tony Barr

45

Directing the Camera

You will work closely with the Director of Photography to figure out the overall look of the Film. You may want to tell your DP what emotion you would like to convey when discussing the Shot List and/or Storyboards. They may (and hopefully will) suggest things that you haven't thought of to help communicate that emotion with the Camera, such as using simple techniques like placement (High, Low or Dutch Angle, etc.) or suggesting when a Close-Up (CU) might be most effective.

    The casual moviegoer may not fully comprehend why they feel a certain way in a Scene, but subtle conventions can have a lot to do with that. Like so many aspects of Filmmaking, it is tied into a psychological response. For this reason it's important to get either the Shot List or Storyboards to the DP well in advance so that you can discuss and revise before the shoot day, and so you can break down each Scene in greater detail beforehand.

    It's also important to know what you have at your disposal as far as any special Camera Support equipment (Camera Stabilizer, Dolly, Jib/Crane, Drone, etc.) and for which Scenes. There might be limitations to the Location itself (remoteness, no-fly zone, etc.) that calls for only certain types of Shots, and it's important to be aware of these when designing them. Most narrative Films are shot Single-Camera, but there are certain situations–such as Stunts, Explosions or any Scenes where extra Takes would be difficult–that multiple Cameras may be utilized.

    Try to balance your time between looking at a Monitor feed of what's on Camera–designed so that you're not constantly peering into the Viewfinder or over your DP's shoulder–and watching what is happening on Set with your own eyes. Learning when to focus and what to fix your attention on is a key to Directing, and can be more difficult at times than it seems.

    Develop a working rhythm when calling "Action"

and "Cut" so that everyone involved can focus on the important nuances of the Shot. And don't be that Director who forgets to turn their phone off and blows a great Take—even if it's a "MOS" Shot, it can still be distracting.

If you are doing your own Camera operating (not recommended, especially for novice Directors), just know that you always want to record at the highest quality that is practical. You always want to keep Batteries charged, to avoid any filming delays. And make sure Media is formatted beforehand and stored safely after being recorded onto until the Footage is transferred. It's a lot to learn, and if you're not that technical I highly suggest getting a friend with a Camera that is comfortable shooting with it, and has a good eye for Composition and can keep subjects in Focus at the very least.

Consider renting a Camera to shoot at a higher quality than is otherwise available to you in your circle. Even better, hire a DP that has their own Camera package that they are familiar with. Most legitimate DPs have access to a Camera of preference for a decent price, so be sure to consult with them first.

Recommended Reading:
- *Setting Up Your Shots* by Jeremy Vineyard
- *Cinematography* by Kris Malkiewicz
- *The Five C's of Cinematography* by Joseph V. Mascelli

Online Resources:
- *Directors Guild of America* (www.dga.org)
- *The American Society of Cinematographers* (www.theasc.com)

Continuity & Coverage

Shooting for Continuity and getting Coverage are two of the biggest things to always make sure to do as a Director.

Continuity simply means that your Shots will cut together from one to the next, ensuring that certain performances, Props and/or additional elements have a continuous feel to them all after being Edited together. The Script Supervisor will be your best friend in this regard, if you are lucky enough to find an experienced one. They will have a Script Log where they jot all kinds of notes down in shorthand, later giving you a report that is typed up. They must use their shorthand when on Set because things move so quickly at times and they must not slow down the Production. If a Director forgets which hand the Actor used in any given Action, the Script Supervisor should have a note of it. This is usually a quicker option than playing back the Footage, which can slow down the pace of shooting if relied on too heavily.

Coverage is making sure you get enough solid Takes from enough Angles "in the can" to be able to cut the Scene together without any Jump Cuts (unless used intentionally as a technique). The best way to ensure Coverage is to use Master Scene Technique, which involves starting on a Wide Shot (if applicable) and working your way "Out to In" getting your Medium then Close-Ups and Inserts/Cutaways. This is a tried and true method that a Director should be familiar with, whether it is utilized in every Scene or not. Also, be aware of "The 180-Degree Rule", as this has a big effect on the Screen Direction and Eyeline of your subjects.

Knowing that you have enough Takes to work with is like having an additional sense that an experienced Director develops over time. This sense develops much faster for Directors who Edit their own work as well. It's always good to shoot a few extra Takes when in doubt, as it's easier to roll while all set up than try to pick up any Shots later. You will thank yourself for developing this good habit when you get into the Editing room.

Pickups and Re-shoots end up costing much more money, and for a low-budget Production it could mean the difference between a finished or incomplete project. Take pride in getting what you need during Principal Photography without resorting to Pickups and Reshoots, and your Producers will thank you!

Recommended Reading:
- *Film Directing: Shot by Shot* by Steven D. Katz
- *Making Movies* by Sidney Lumet

Lighting

Although Cameras have gotten better in terms of Exposure and Sensitivity in low-light in recent years, Lighting is still a big part of the Filmmaking process and probably always will be. This is because the manipulation of Light can invoke a completely different feeling in the Scene, can create interest and, at the risk of sounding sinister, can manipulate the viewer in certain ways without them realizing.

Along with Cameras having better Sensors, the lights themselves have gotten smaller in size, and the "old school" Production people out there will always be quick to comment, much cooler (old Movie lights were blazing hot!). LED lights have become the latest choice because they are efficient, compact and stay cool. Fluorescents are a decent option too, but are quickly losing market share to LEDs. The big, heavy 10K or 5K (K=one thousand watts!) Tungsten Halogen and even HMIs have yielded to newer, more efficient technologies. But many were built like tanks while putting out an incredible amount of light and therefore still exist.

This is all stuff that you will be working on closely with your DP, as well as with a Gaffer (Lead Electrician) and other Department Heads such as Art Director and/or Production Designer where applicable.

For complicated Lighting setups, it's best to come up with a Lighting Diagram with your Director of

Photography and Gaffer. This way everybody knows which Lights to set up where, and any power concerns can be addressed well in advance. Again it's about having a plan that everybody can start to visualize and discuss if needed.

I come from the school of "less is more" in the realm of Lighting and like to shoot on Cameras that give a lot of latitude that way. If a naturalistic approach is something that works to complement the Story, then go with it. Maybe you will only need Practicals, Reflectors, and Bounce Cards in that case.

Novice Directors tend to get intimidated by Lighting, or just do a terrible job at it, and this is where having a solid DP will do wonders. As a bonus, they usually have fun toys such as Light Meters, Dimmers, Snoots, Gobos, etc. A good DP should have a grasp of at least being able to get you a decent Exposure on every Shot, and hopefully with your input will design some well-lit, visually interesting Scenes.

Recommended Reading:
- *Film Lighting* by Kris Malkiewicz
- *Single-Camera Video Production* by Robert B. Musburger

Online Resources:
- *Lighting Diagram* (www.lightingdiagram.com)
- *Kino Flo Lighting Systems* (www.kinoflo.com)

Sound Recordist

Since the invention of "Talkies," recording good Sound on a Film Set has been an exciting innovation that has its own set of challenges and unique Crew member(s) to handle it properly.

As with most departments, the size of the Sound Crew will depend on the scale of the overall Production and its specific needs. Of course first and foremost is that there is Dialogue to begin with. I specify "Dialogue" because it has become increasingly easier to get a wide selection of high quality Sound FX for a nominal monthly membership or even à la carte. Gone are the days where people had to carry huge Sound Libraries around, hoping they had what they needed contained on those precious discs. All but obsolete are the days when Foley Artists are needed to recreate Sounds such as footsteps and punches.

Because of these advances in Sound Design (discussed further in the Post-Production section), it affords you the ability to shoot much more quickly overall, perhaps only needing to roll Sound during Shots involving Dialogue and building the rest of the Soundtrack in Post-Production.

There are several ways to record Dialogue depending on the type of Shot. The traditional method involves using a Boom Mic setup. The current process is to have the Boom Mic running directly into a small digital recorder. The Sound recorded is then synced up in the Edit, which is referred to as Double-System Recording. This is where a Clapboard (aka Slate) comes into use—to sync the Video with the Audio.

Nowadays the equipment is simple enough that the same person can usually Boom and Mix on a small Set. Sometimes a handheld Pistol-Grip is used in tighter situations where a Boom Mic is not practical. The same Double-System concept can be applied to a wireless Lavalier Mic hidden carefully on your Actors so they can still move around without making rustling noises on the track.

Holding on a Take for the rumble of an airplane or far off noise that only the Microphone can pick up is common. Just plan on needing a few extra Takes when running Sound, and for the overall pace of shooting to slow down. Also make sure that you have somebody with a good ear that is dedicated to getting you clean Audio you

51

can use later. They should remember to get a Room Tone track for each Interior Scene: 30-60 seconds of "empty" Sound with the Crew present, to lay down as a base in Editing so that Dialogue lines don't awkwardly stand out in the Mix. They should also keep track of any pickups (aka Wild Lines) of Dialogue that may have been interfered with by Action.

It's really no fun to need to call Actors back for ADR (Automatic Dialogue Replacement), which is a misnomer because there is nothing "automatic" about it. Just try your best to get clean, usable Sound on Set. And somebody should be listening through Headphones as well as watching Signal Levels at all times. Enough said.

Recommended Reading:

- *Production Sound Mixing* by John J. Murphy

Stunts & Firearms

I have mentioned aspects of safety previously, but something to be particularly aware of is a situation where you are putting people in even the most remote risk of danger. This would primarily be while doing Stunts and/or using Firearms, even those that are plugged and don't shoot Blanks.

I highly advise hiring a Stunt Coordinator for those Scenes that need it, with the approach that you would like to shoot Green Screen wherever it's feasible. This way you can have Stunts on vehicles that aren't even moving, or shoot dynamic perspectives without any real danger. The Stunt Coordinator along with your Visual FX Supervisor will be your go-to Department Heads for how to pull off any of these Scenes. You will save all sorts of time and headaches by taking their advice. A good Stunt Coordinator should know how to stage the Action and when it's best to use the Actor, Stunt Performer or even a Dummy.

While shooting Firearms with Blanks on a Film Set was once a necessity, you can now use easily created (and/or downloaded) digital muzzle flashes and Sound FX which can be added in Post-Production. Airsoft guns are incredibly realistic and only shoot soft foam bullets, and foam Prop guns are great for fight Scenes because nobody risks getting hit with metal. Just stay away from Blank Guns altogether if you can. But it still makes sense to have a Firearms Expert on Set to show proper handling techniques since there is still risk of injury, however slight, with using Airsoft and Prop guns. Firearms Experts will also be able to consult on other believability aspects for performances.

It's also important if you will be running around with Prop guns and making loud noises (from any sort of Squibs or Pyrotechnics going off) that you alert all the surrounding neighbors. Even with the proper permission, it will save time and hassle and any chance at false alarms to communicate what you are doing clearly to the surrounding residences and/or businesses beforehand.

Recommended Reading:
- *The DV Rebel's Guide* by Stu Maschwitz

Online Resources:
- *New Rule FX* (www.newrulefx.com)

Special Effects

Special Effects are physical, On-Camera illusions that need to be built beforehand (how much lead time is dictated by the complexity of the Effect), and overseen by a Special Effects Supervisor. Common elements include Animatronics, Pyrotechnics, Miniatures or complicated Prosthetic Makeup. Together these are also known as Practical Effects.

The Special Effects Supervisor will in turn work with

the Visual FX Supervisor to determine what can be accomplished On-Camera (filmed during Production) or what would work best as Computer-Generated Imagery (CGI), added during Post-Production. Several factors enter in to this decision such as Budget, Schedule and safety issues.

Striking the correct balance between Special Effects and Visual FX is usually the key to an effect-laden Movie these days. On a small Production, the Special Effects Supervisor and Visual FX Supervisor may be one and the same.

More is discussed regarding Visual FX in Post-Production, since that is the stage at which it will be completed, but it is usually helpful to get both your Special Effects and Visual FX person involved early in Pre-Production if you have a Film that will rely heavily on such elements.

In budgetary terms, Animals fall under Special Effects so I will briefly mention them here. Animal Handlers are a specialized occupation but can be found outside of Hollywood—in pet stores, zoos or sanctuaries. If you need one be sure to book them in advance. Again I will stress respect and safety for every living thing on Set. The correct mix of Live Action, CGI and Puppetry can create any necessary illusions without endangering the Actors, human or otherwise.

Recommended Reading:
- *Scare Tactics* by John Russo
- *The ASC Treasury of Visual Effects* by George E. Turner

Still Photos

It used to be an absolute must to hire a Still Photographer if you wanted any sort of visual record of what happens Behind-The-Scenes on a Shoot. Gone are the days when simply taking Photos demanded its own level of expertise. But if your Budget allows, it is still worth it to hire a professional Still Photographer, at least for the biggest days of the Shoot.

A good Still Photographer will have an innate knack for getting great candid and Behind-The-Scenes shots without interrupting the flow of the Shoot (and hopefully never ruining a Take with the click or flash of the Camera). They will get a unique perspective that the Movie Camera just won't be capable of capturing because the focus (no pun intended) will be on the subject matter of the Movie, not the Shoot itself.

Although it's much more feasible to grab a high-Resolution freeze frame for a Poster or even Billboard Promo nowadays, it's usually beneficial to have the Behind-The-Scenes coverage provided by a Still Photographer as well. When it comes time to market the Movie, you will want every creative option possible at your disposal.

A note on the amount of control that you want to exert over Cast, Crew and visitors taking their own Photos and Video (and what they can do with them) in these days of Social Media and Livestreaming: be clear on what your policy is, especially to people coming to your Set for the first time. There might be Scenes that are alright to post compared to Scenes that are critical to Plot elements that must stay hidden from the public eye. A happy medium can be struck by letting people know that they are free to snap Photos and Video but can only post them after the Film has been released. Whatever your policy is, make sure it is clear, consistent and in writing!

Recommended Reading:
- *Read This If You Want to Take Great Photographs* by Henry Carroll

Staying On Schedule

Staying on Schedule while in Production is so critical that it needs to be re-emphasized here. The Schedule has so many factors involved that bumping a Scene to shoot at a later date is sometimes just not an option. That's why it's not only important to stay on top of the daily Schedule, but the overall Schedule as well, to understand how they are inevitably tied together.

There are several tricks to staying on Schedule. One is to have your Shot List ordered into the Shots for the day, and really think through all factors and possibilities beforehand. This technique gives your subconscious time to work on possible extras and solutions within this Schedule, and it can give you some of the best creative surprises.

Another big time-saver when you're feeling the pressure and running a bit behind is to find ways to combine Shots. Oftentimes we tend to "over-direct" on our Shot List, but once we get out there we realize that plenty of coverage can be obtained using fewer Setups. Focusing on Staging and Blocking a Scene properly and deciding the best primary Camera placement can lead to less of a need for cutting and therefore less Shots/Setups for the day.

Rather than starting and stopping to re-slate the Camera on Close-Ups and Inserts, it can save shooting time if performed in a Series of Takes where the Camera remains rolling throughout. Be sure to label it as such on the Slate and Script Notes so that the Editor will know what you did.

When assessing the overall Schedule, it's important to see how Locations might be combined (i.e., shoot one Scene in a room at a Location and shoot a completely different Scene in another area). Also having Cover Locations that you can shoot alternate Scenes in when the weather is bad gives you flexibility and is a typical backup plan for Exterior Scene days. These Cover Locations are usually places that can be filmed at on short notice and at any time (like a Producer's house or something similar) and become Plan B for shooting during any adverse weather.

Sometimes the most creative solutions come out of the simple necessity of staying on Schedule. Have a plan, but be ready for it to change on the fly. Force your mind to go through the visualization exercises, even if the end result will be slightly different. Just try not to sacrifice quality or process as you go. Getting sloppy on Set will inevitably lead to a lot of time fixing things in Post (and throw that Schedule off), so keep your wits about you even when things get hectic. And they will, guaranteed!

Recommended Reading:
- *The Beginning Filmmaker's Guide to a Successful First Film* by Renee Harmon & Jim Lawrence

Staying On Budget

Working with a Production Budget requires constant adjustment (much like the Schedule), as budgetary issues will arise with even the most experienced Line Producer and Production Manager overseeing the bottom line.

The main thing to be aware of here is how to make important choices in a rational manner while trying to balance the product On-Screen and not overworking the Crew or skimping on "amenities." You will be forced to make creative decisions for budgetary reasons, and they will not always be easy ones to make.

Knowing what you need in order to tell your Story (and which the "wish list" items are) is critical and must be thought through if and when the circumstances arise. The art of compromise is also in full effect, because as all Budgets go, where you draw extra for one department then others must be cut. Communication is important, especially when it's bad news that must be conveyed.

Any major Budget decisions should be discussed in a meeting whenever possible, as things can get misconstrued via email and other communications. It's really a chance to work through a creative solution as a team rather than debating it as Department Heads. If you can create that sort of atmosphere then you're on the right track.

Recommended Reading:

- *What They Don't Teach You at Film School* by Camille Landau and Tiare White

Overcoming Adversity

Making a Feature Film really is a marathon, not a sprint. It requires an extraordinary amount of persistence, which is a much more measurable and objective trait than the slippery term known as "talent." If I had to choose one over the other, persistence would win every time. Every "talented" Filmmaker gets tested at times by adversity. How they deal with that adversity is oftentimes the determining factor as to whether they have a future in this business. Talent is a bonus that may ultimately set your work apart from the pack if and when it's completed, but persistence is what will get it finished.

If you have made it through the end of Production (or at least Principal Photography), you can breathe a sigh of relief. The bulk of your physical work is done, and it's time for a whole different reality: one where you will see the fruits of your labors come together and learn all new lessons in Post-Production.

Recommended Reading:

- *Rebel Without a Crew* by Robert Rodriguez
- *Shooting to Kill* by Christine Vachon
- *My First Movie* by Stephen Lowenstein

PART 4
POST-PRODUCTION SIMPLIFIED

Editing

On a basic level, the process of Editing a Film is simply arranging what you have shot into a logical order to tell the Story. However Editing is a craft all of its own. How a Scene is cut together can add emotion, suspense, or comedy where it wasn't apparent in the Raw Footage. It can save sub-par Acting performances and fix technical issues. Most importantly, Editing sets the overall pace and rhythm of your Film through the rising and falling Action within each Scene.

Nowadays most Filmmakers try to get a jump on the Editing process while still in Production as this helps give them an idea of how the Film is taking shape. Cutting together some "Dailies" can be a great learning tool as well.

The Script will be your creative road map, and the Script Supervisor's Notes will be your key to the technical side of things. Without these two documents, telling a cohesive Story that will be technically solid is nearly impossible, or at least much more ambiguous and time-consuming. These two documents are on my desk at all times as I Edit, scratching notes on my already annotated Script and trying to decipher the Script Supervisor's Notes that can be a bit complex at times.

When creating a new project, take time to make sure all the settings are optimized, and organize your Assets into Bins (Footage, Titles, etc.). Your files for the project should ideally be located in a single folder (preferably on an external high-capacity RAID Hard Drive Array) and saved alongside the Project File itself. Choose a Sequence preset that matches your Footage as close as possible. Save your progress early and often as Editing systems pushed to their limits will crash at times! It's also smart to have a backup of the Project File in case it gets corrupted or deleted somehow.

After that it's a matter of finding and marking the best Shots and Takes by skimming through the Raw Footage and making notes on any usable bits in-between. A good Editor will watch every last frame of Footage, albeit often-times at a high speed if the Shots and Takes are clearly marked. Learning the keyboard shortcuts for your chosen Editing Software is a necessity. Taking notes will save all kinds of time and confusion later on when you are in the visual flow of Editing and using the other side of your brain.

Beyond that, different types of Films have different workflows. It may be wise to set up several Sequences depending on the length of the Film, as it's easier to work in shorter pieces and then assemble them together later in a Master Sequence. If the piece is Narration-driven, it may make sense to cut the Narration together first to develop the rhythm and then cut the visuals in later. If the Film or Sequence is very Music-driven, it might make sense to lay down some Music tracks first and cut in visuals Montage-style. If it's Documentary or Reality style, a Selects Reel (of the best Footage) might be an optimal starting point.

There are several similarities and connections between the Writing and Editing processes. Much like the first draft of your Script, the First Assembly should be raw and unrefined. It doesn't make any sense to spend a bunch of time fine-tuning Shots that are going to change drastically in duration or may not even make the Final Cut, so don't bother. There will be plenty of time for refining later, trust me on that one.

For a scripted Film, the Assembly Edit (aka "Rough Cut") should try to reflect the revised Script as much as possible. Scenes change and evolve into their own entities later, but what was written on the page should closely reflect what's on the screen.

Getting the Assembly Edit done is always a relief as it is that moment that you know you have a Film. From there it's all about making it better, constantly trying to view it through the lens of the audience and making sure that it communicates your vision. This is really hard for one person to do objectively, especially if you are the Writer and the Director as well as the Editor, so it's very important to pull in other sets of eyes during this process. First and foremost, always trust your own gut instinct, but also have another Producer (or at least your friend or family member that is a big Movie buff) watch each Scene for certain things that you may be uncertain about.

Is a certain Character's introduction as clear as it should be? Is the point of a particular Scene apparent within the Structure of the Plot? Could an Actor's performance be improved by finding a better take of a certain line? Do you linger too much on that beautiful Establishing Shot and should you cut away from it sooner? These are just a few of the things that an Editor must consider.

Suggested Software:
- *Adobe Premiere Pro*
- *Avid Media Composer*
- *Apple Final Cut Pro*

Recommended Reading:
- *On Film Editing* by Edward Dmytryk
- *In the Blink of an Eye* by Walter Murch
- *Cut by Cut* by Gael Chandler

Online Resources:
- *Lynda* (www.lynda.com) – tutorials
- *Film Editing Pro* (www.filmeditingpro.com) – tutorials

Color Correction

Color Correction (aka Color Timing) is a tedious and technical rather than creative process, but there's really no way around it. Inevitably, the Camera(s) you used to capture your Movie will not always match, even from one Shot to the next. There are a lot of reasons for this: Color Temperature shift, Exposure or Lighting change, or just plain electronic inconsistencies. Whatever the case is, you must get these Shots to look consistent, especially within a particular Scene.

Some preliminary Color Correction may happen during the Editing stage just to make things a bit more watchable and make certain that a Shot will work at all. It is highly recommended that you establish Picture Lock (i.e., no more Shot or timing changes in the Edit) before the deep dive in the Color Correction stage happens.

It is crucial to do Color Correction at this point because the next few visual steps are creative and will allow you to focus on those aspects once you're at that stage. Get familiar with Video Scopes and Color Wheels and the relationships of all the Tools (most if not all of which can be found in your Editing Software) and what they are and are not capable of achieving.

I usually work methodically, starting at the beginning of the Film and adjusting each shot's Brightness, Contrast, Color Balance, etc. according to the provided Video Scopes (Waveform Monitors for Luminance, Black and White Levels and Vectorscopes for Hue, Saturation and Color information). Always Color Correct to skin tones whenever possible, as these inconsistencies are obvious and therefore distracting when they don't match from Shot to Shot.

It helps at some point, when you think you have it all dialed in, to watch the Film on a completely different monitor and playback system so long as it has a trusted picture. I usually burn a Disc and watch it on my TV to find potential errors before moving on.

Suggested Software:
- *Adobe Premiere Pro* (Lumetri Plug-In)
- *Blackmagic DaVinci Resolve*

Recommended Reading:
- *Color Correction Handbook* by Alexis Van Hurkman

Online Resources:
- *Udemy* (www.udemy.com) – courses

Visual FX

Visual FX have always been a part of the Filmmaking process, but digital technology has made them much cheaper and easier to execute. Of course it still takes an expert with a trained eye to pull off even the simplest Computer-Generated Imagery (CGI) Effects and make them believable to the discerning audiences of the 21st century, especially at increasingly higher Resolutions.

Uses of Visual FX can be subtle, such as replacing an Actor's eye Color to match a certain physical description, or creating a cityscape in a distant window using a Green or Blue Screen (what used to be accomplished using a Scenic Matte Painting). Or they can be more complex and involve a combination of Practical (what should have been filmed already) and Digital FX to help sell the illusion. They can even be fully Animated Sequences using a combination of techniques such as 2D Cel or Hand Drawn, 3D, and Stop-Motion. Please note that entirely Animated Films have different workflows than a Live Action Movie, and it is highly specialized work.

The Visual FX stage seems to be the place where an inexperienced or overly ambitious Filmmaker's project bogs down and is in constant danger of coming to a standstill. One simple rule is to get the Visual FX Artist involved with the project early, before the shoot. An experienced Visual FX Artist will give you invaluable input as to how to pull off certain Shots, and they will work closely with the Special Effects Supervisor (or may be the same person). They can also begin the process of creating any CGI Effects early on so that you're not stuck waiting too long for the Visual FX Artist to put the finishing touches on.

While it's feasible to "farm out" certain tasks in Visual FX these days (even overseas to Render Farms), it is important to think about both the technical and artistic elements and what a truly talented Visual FX Artist can mean to your team. This is ultimately decided by two things: the first is Budget (that evil word that we all love to hate), and the other is how good of a fit their style is to that particular Film. Look at their Reel of past work similar to how you would when hiring a Director of Photography.

If you're crazy enough as a first time Filmmaker to try to do all the Visual FX yourself, just be prepared for a steep learning curve (such as in learning at least two or three more Software programs), probably a computer upgrade if you don't have a screaming fast system, and also for the possibility of failure in this regard. I'm just telling it like it is. If your piece is dramatic and your Visual FX look cartoonish because you're not really a Visual FX Artist, it has the potential to ruin certain Scenes, if not the Movie as a whole.

Suggested Software:
- *Adobe After Effects*
- *Cinema 4D*
- *PFTrack*

Recommended Reading:
- *The Visual Effects Arsenal* by Bill Byrne

Online Resources:

- *FXPHD* (www.fxphd.com) – online training

Color Grading

Whereas the objective in Color Correction is to make the image look good on a technical level, Color Grading is the creative side of the equation.

Color Grading comes with its own set of challenges, but if you put in the time on the Color Correction side of things beforehand, then your job will be much simpler, more creative (and more fun!) on the Color Grading end.

Color can represent different emotions in Film, even giving us subconscious hints as to Time, Place, Character or Plot. Knowing how to manipulate these elements is an artform in itself, and applying Color to them correctly can be crucial to the success of your Movie. In the digital era it is much simpler to capture a rather "flat" image in terms of Color palette and liven it up immensely in Post-Production.

Nowadays it really is amazing what can be accomplished in Color Grading with some Presets on certain Plug-Ins. If you have a pro level Plug-In package (which I highly recommend obtaining because it will set your work apart), it can be as simple as applying one of these Presets, then tweaking a few Slider settings and finding the visual look you are going for, or one that brings something entirely new to the Scene.

If you don't have the eye for Color Grading or the technical skills to do it yourself, hire somebody with the experience and specialized workstation as your Colorist to help complete this critical yet under-appreciated piece of the puzzle. Be prepared to sit in with them, spending hours on end staring at a Scene you may already be sick of, and try to do it with fresh eyes.

If you are working remotely, make sure to get plenty of Color samples for approval before starting the time-consuming process of rendering the final Color Grading.

Suggested Software:
- *Red Giant* – Plug-Ins for Adobe, Apple & Avid
- *Boris FX* – Plug-Ins for Adobe, Apple, Avid & OFX

Recommended Reading:
- *Color Correction Look Book* by Alexis Van Hurkman

Online Resources:
- *Learn Color Grading* (www.learncolorgrading.com)

Sound Design

Sound Design is another under-appreciated part of the Post-Production process, but a little effort goes a long way. Much can be done with Sound Design to make your Film seem "bigger" than it really is, enhance the emotions of what is happening on-screen, or add a whole different element to the finished product.

To put it simply, the Sound Designer is responsible for the layering of any Sound that isn't the Musical Score. This includes Dialogue, which should have been recorded On-Location, and any ADR (Automatic Dialogue Recording). Be sure to give the Sound Designer notes on the Script and your vision for any requests on specific Shots or Scenes. This will allow the Sound Designer to work efficiently in a creative space, having everything they need to begin building the layers of Sound.

Sound Design can be fairly simple and minimalist, or it can be very complex to fit the needs of the Production. If you have a Character-driven period drama, a sparse Sound Design may be more appropriate. If you made a sci-fi Film that is supposed to take place on a spaceship, it may be much more complex.

It's amazing what is available in online Sound FX

libraries for a nominal membership fee, and coming into a Session with a hard drive full of high-quality, royalty-free files will put a smile on any Sound Designer's face. Even FX that used to require a Foley studio, such as footsteps or other subtleties that are rarely captured in Production but can enhance certain details of the Story, are now available in these online libraries.

It is also at this point that any and all Voice-over (V.O.) recording needs to be finalized. Be sure to record a clean Audio track in a studio-quality environment and using a high-quality microphone—it will make all the difference in the end.

Sound Designers will find all the layers and pieces of Sound and put them in the proper place on a Timeline with the cut of your Film. This is essentially prepping it for the final Sound Mix, which will come after the Musical Score or Soundtrack has been added by the Composer and/or Music Supervisor.

Suggested Software:
- *Avid ProTools*
- *Adobe Audition*

Recommended Reading:
- *Sound Design* by David Sonnenschein

Online Resources:
- *AudioBlocks* (www.audioblocks.com)

Music

Musical Scores have the power to make or break the entire feeling of a Movie. They can enhance or even create a mood in a Scene, giving the audience important emotional cues on how to interpret what they are seeing visually. The Musical Score is usually instrumental and relatively nonintrusive, with many modern Composers taking more of a minimalist approach depending upon the Genre of the Film.

This is also another stage where your Film can be delayed weeks or months if you haven't planned ahead and communicated your vision to a Composer. The earlier you can get a Picture Lock cut to a Composer, the better. Even giving them Rough Cuts (making sure they know the timing isn't final!) can allow them to develop movements and Themes based on the emotions of each Scene.

Usually while Editing I lay in several "scratch tracks" which are pieces of Copyrighted music that I borrow to help me set a rhythm or tone to a Scene. I will then share them with the Composer as examples of what I'm looking for. This takes the guess work out of the equation for the Composer as far as what mood I am trying to set, and they usually appreciate the input since it saves them time and energy. The Musical Score can be quite a subjective item and therefore difficult to verbalize or nail down without examples.

There are Royalty-Free (Stock) music options which allow you basically to act as your own Music Supervisor. But there are plenty of talented Composers willing to work for below market value in order to get exposure, especially if your Film has the potential to be a hit. Having the personal touch of an experienced Composer will give your Movie another layer of uniqueness, and is highly encouraged. No need to worry about being located in an area where Composers may be scarce, as this is a task that can definitely be accomplished working remotely.

If you have a background in Music, it may be wisest to get a Keyboard or your best Instrument and create your own Music Cues à la John Carpenter or Robert Rodriguez. You may just find the right tone for your piece and save quite a bit on the Budget.

Another option is to use a Soundtrack with popular Music, by either securing the rights to already recorded songs or having Musicians record brand-new material for the Movie. If you're going this route of recording from the ground up, just know that it will take more lead time, money, and effort than it would simply to secure the rights to a batch of little-known songs. However, you also then own the rights to what you have recorded and can release it as a Soundtrack, either to promote the Film or as an additional revenue stream (or both!).

If you are lucky enough to be working with a large Budget, you may be able to secure the rights to some of your favorite songs. In this case, I would advise going straight to the Music Publishing Company rather than the Artist or Band. It begins to get complicated in terms of legalities and Royalties when dealing with major Record Labels, but if your Film absolutely has to have a certain piece of popular Music, just be willing to pay dearly for it. On a similar note, make sure to avoid writing and shooting a Scene that will be completely dependent on a specific piece of Music for it to work, unless you get the rights to the Music beforehand.

Suggested Software:
- *Avid ProTools*
- *Apple Logic*

Recommended Reading:
- *Music Composition for Film and Television* by Lalo Schifrin

Online Resources:
- *The American Society of Composers, Authors and Publishers* (www.ascap.com)
- *Musicbed* (www.musicbed.com)

Sound Mix

A professional Sound Mix is an essential part of the

process for any Feature Film or anything that is going to be screened in a Theater, even just once. Amplifying Sound brings out every little detail and mistake, so it's essential to get the Sound Mix polished over by a professional with an ear for every issue as well as the skills to be able to fix those issues.

Once every element has been laid in to the final Sequence and there will be no more timing changes, the Sound Mixer can begin their process. It is a primarily technical process that will need a surprising amount of creative input, so plan on spending several nights on the Sound Mix.

There are ways to complete this process remotely of course, and if you are a great communicator and willing to accept the Sound Mixer's interpretation, the process can be accomplished this way. Many Sound Mixers prefer to work remotely (especially if the pay rate is low) because it allows them the flexibility to work on the Mix during down-times in their studio.

Make sure you are clear on the workflow during this stage, and be ready to create special Exports of the final (Video) Sequences for the Sound Mixer to work from. Pay close attention to their instructions for prepping the Mix, as it will save headaches when having the Sound Mixer open your files. They will also ask you technical questions such as your preference on Mastering in special formats, which applies for either Theatrical screenings or Digital Distribution. It's very possible that you will want several versions of the Final Sound Mix and it's important to have that discussion with your Producing Team beforehand.

You should get your Final Sound Mix as a high-quality stereo Master File so that it can be synced up with the picture for a Final Export. Also make sure that you get a copy of all Project Files so that if you need to go back and create other versions of Mixes (for foreign Distribution etc.) those will be available to you. This will prevent trouble down the road and will give you more flexibility in working with another Sound Mixer (if need be) to make a Distribution deadline.

Suggested Software:
- *Avid ProTools*
- *Apple Logic*
- *Adobe Audition*

Recommended Reading:
- *Audio in Media* by Stanley R. Alten

Online Resources:
- *ProSoundWeb* (www.prosoundweb.com)

Final Export

Once you have your Picture Lock cut and Final Sound Mix, it's time to do what will hopefully be the Final Export of your files for a Test Screening at least. Somewhere along the line you will have been working on a Title Design for both your Opening and Closing Movie Credits and you will incorporate this together with the Film if you haven't already. It's best to wait as long as you can to finalize Titles, to make sure all Post-Production Crew is included. Make sure to include everybody that helped, no matter how large or small of a role. And proofread your Titles! It's not only a matter of professional courtesy, but can actually be a legal issue. Even if you have Errors and Omissions Insurance to cover you, do your best to get all Credits correct and accurate.

A good rule of thumb is that your Final Export should be the same Resolution and Bit-Rate as the format you shot your Movie on. If you shot on several Cameras, it's always best to go with the highest Resolution format. Any data beyond this is just a waste of space since it will never be higher Resolution than your Source Material, anyway. You will be taking this high-quality

Master (or Masters, depending upon Deliverables), and making any lower-Resolution files by Encoding from the Master File.

Final Export can be done either directly out of the Editing Software or through a supporting Compression program which can also handle it–sometimes provide more Presets, etc. Encoding of files for online Streaming, Disc and other formats are best handled by programs specifically designed for that task. Encoding programs offer better quality and usually more control than the Editing or Compression Software will.

At this point you will surely be tired of watching your inevitable masterpiece, but you must view every last frame of the Master File and make sure there are no Glitches or Pixelation issues. You will also want to make sure that the Sound is crisp and clean and is synced up to the Video as well. Once you have done a quality control check of your Movie and have a clean Master File, it's time for the nerve-wracking yet all-important Test Screening.

Suggested Software:
- *Adobe Premiere Pro/Media Encoder*
- *Handbrake*

Online Resources:
- *Larry Jordan* (www.larryjordan.com)
- *DVCreators* (www.dvcreators.net)

Test Screening

A private Test Screening is always a good idea, even if it's under the guise of a sneak preview for Cast, Crew and Investors. It will make all the people that worked on the Movie feel good to be the first to see their own work, and although they may not exactly be objective about things, they will be sure to point out technical issues if they think their contributions could be presented better.

It's also advised to have a few local Film buffs (but not the media!) in the crowd, people whose opinion you trust and that had minimal or no involvement in the Movie. Listen to them for input on Story and Character elements, especially if they noticed any flaws or shortcomings.

Rent a screen at a local Movie Theater or multi-use space that is big enough to accommodate at least those that worked on the Movie and hopefully several more. Even if you're offered another kind of space, don't host it at a business or private residence. The technical requirements won't be nearly as good, not to mention that it's just unprofessional.

Retain the services of the on-site Projectionist, or hire your own. Keep the popcorn and refreshments flowing (for free!), as it will make for a happier audience. And make sure to factor these expenses into your Marketing Budget from the get-go. Splurge where you can. Show some effort and decorate the place as the Cast and Crew will appreciate it.

Have a good Microphone with amplified Sound, and be sure to have a brief introduction, thanking the Cast, Crew, Investors and everybody that helped. You should also plan for a Q&A session afterward. You will be able to tell if your audience is downright confused about anything through their tone of voice and through the types of questions they ask. It is also great practice for future Screenings where the audience might not be so friendly toward your creative choices or sensibilities.

Everybody should be given an anonymous questionnaire before they start watching the Film, and make sure to collect as many of these as possible before everybody leaves at the end. They may be smiling and congratulatory about getting the Movie finished, as this is an accomplishment in and of itself, but the questionnaires will be your best bet for honest feedback from the night.

If you get a bunch of critical notes on a fixable aspect

of the Film, it is well worth considering making changes. Just know that if you do so, you will need the time of a few Post-Production Crew members at the very least, and it can drive the Budget up quickly to make additional changes. In the end it's always best to take all feedback with a grain of salt, but also not be too stubborn. Little fixes can go a long way toward making drastic improvements to a Movie.

However, if you feel that the Test Screening was a success and you are confident that your Film will play well to a larger audience, it is now time to prepare your materials for the final phase of the Filmmaking process: Distribution.

Online Resources:

- *Gofobo* (www.gofobo.com)
- *Advance Screenings* (www.advancescreenings.com)

PART 5
DISTRIBUTION SIMPLIFIED

Developing a Marketing Plan

By this time you should really know who you made this
Movie for (i.e., the Target Audience). You will need to
attempt to reach them in areas where they will be
searching for what's new. For older audiences, advertising
in print magazines, the newspaper, and on daytime TV
might work. For a younger crowd, it's all about getting
people to your Website and Social Media pages.

At this point you should at least come up with a
Teaser Graphic and preferably a Teaser Trailer to
match. You will use this as the Movie's primary Artwork
until a full Poster design is created. This goes for the
Teaser Trailer as well, although sometimes it is just easier
to create a full Trailer, and then cut several Teasers from
that. Or you can create a Trailer using a brief Scene that is
a key moment in the Story, which can be produced rather
quickly and cheaply since most of the work is already
done.

Use the Assets created from the Teaser Poster then
buy a domain name reflecting your Movie's Title,
and launch a Website. Or if your Production Company
has a site, just add a page to it with the Teaser Trailer and
any key information and/or credits for your Film. This
Website will become a landing place for all future
information on the Movie and should be tied to all
relevant Social Media elements as well.

At some point in this process you will want to hire a
Publicist/PR Firm. They are worth the price for their
industry connections alone. But make sure that they have
these before hiring them on!

Their first responsibility will usually be to make sure
that your Promotional Materials are top-notch. The
Publicist/PR Firm will help write the all-important Press

Release for your Film and contact various media outlets to spread the word. Busy journalists will generally sample from the Press Release rather than call you for a unique scoop on the Movie since they just need to fill their papers with content. Until your Movie starts winning major awards or garnering other press, it's really not worth their time to interview you. A Press Release–a simple, one-page bulletin that summarizes the Movie and gives bloggers all they need to do a brief write-up of your Film's screening– will help your Movie get the attention it needs.

Then with your Promotional Materials and Marketing Plan firmly in hand, it's time to hit the Film Festival and Film Market circuit.

Recommended Reading:
- *Guerrilla P.R.* by Michael Levine
- *The Publicity Handbook* by David R. Yale with Andrew J. Carothers

Online Resources:
- *Filmmaking Stuff* (www.filmmakingstuff.com)

Film Festivals and Film Markets

Film Festivals can be a great opportunity to screen your Movie in front of an audience. Many independent Films are completed without a planned Theatrical release, as a large percentage of Theaters are more or less dominated by Studio releases these days.

I would generally recommend submitting to as many Film Festivals as possible, especially in these days of cheaper Digital Distribution. However, there are still submission fees for most of them, and some are so new or amateur that they probably aren't worth the time to submit to, let alone attend in person.

Make sure to go after the major Film Festivals first and work your way down the list, as it would give much more publicity for a Premiere if you are lucky enough to secure one of the major Festivals. The next batch of submissions should be to Festivals that specialize in your Genre. At this point (especially if you're finding a hard time getting through the submission process and getting your Film accepted at any Festivals), it would be wise to screen it anywhere you can get it played.

Why is it important to get into a Festival? Because you can start gathering reviews (hopefully positive) from print, Television and Movie industry blogs. You can also see how your Film plays to audiences around the country or world, especially if you're fortunate enough to be able to travel to the Festivals. You can get into a Q&A session and get some press coverage that way, or your Film may win an award at the Festival. Even the smaller Festivals have some talent scouts in attendance on behalf of Agencies, Producers and Studios. If you win awards at the smaller Festivals it makes a better case to get into a larger Festival where the major Theatrical Deals can happen. Beyond that, once it has screened at an approved Festival, it is eligible to be listed on the Internet Movie Database (IMDb) as well–giving it more legitimacy.

After the Film Festival circuit has run its course and you are without a Distribution Deal (or still have territories to sell), it might be wise to get a small Exhibitor Booth at one of the Film Markets, or at least a pass to wander around and speak with potential Distributors. There are relatively few Film Markets and even fewer that are worth paying the Exhibitor fees. This is really where Films get bought and sold, with Distributors from all over the world walking the floor and evaluating what is best for their particular needs. And it may be your Movie's last chance at getting any sort of Theatrical Deal before you would turn to cable & satellite Distribution options.

Recommended Reading:
- *The Film Festival Guide* by Adam Langer
- *The International Film Business* by Angus Finney

Online Resources:
- *Withoutabox* (www.withoutabox.com)
- *FilmFreeway* (www.filmfreeway.com)
- *Festival Focus* (www.festivalfocus.org)
- *American Film Market* (www.americanfilmmarket.com)
- *The Film Catalogue* (www.thefilmcatalogue.com)

Cable & Satellite Distribution

If at this point you have already sold the rights to your Film, then Distribution won't be a concern. But if you're now looking at a Television rather than Theatrical Release, then there are some important things to understand about that part of the business.

Despite the debate over "cord-cutting" (people getting rid of cable or satellite completely), the reality is that some of the largest players in the business are not going anywhere, and the bandwidth still isn't quite there in many regions. That being said, certain pay channels aren't as relevant in the market as they once were since many other basic cable channels can now rival them in quality and selection. The invention of the DVR has made near commercial-free viewing a reality even for those on a busy or irregular schedule.

Think carefully about who might be interested in your Film by studying the content of certain channels. You can do this by using the Digital Guide and searching through a few days' or weeks' worth of content. If you have a Film that fits a specific Genre, it should be an obvious choice. If you submit to some of the more independent and specialized channels, here is where any accolades from your Movie's Festival entries would help sell it to cable and satellite Distributors.

You will have to get through gatekeepers at the Networks, but you should be a pro at handling these types of people by now. If you approach the Networks the right way–through the Query/Pitch letter process–you should get some interest. From there it's just a matter of what their specific programming needs are for the upcoming months.

If you are able to secure a deal with a Network or Video On Demand (VOD), it will greatly boost your Film's potential audience and awareness of it, leading to the possibility of more sales through Disc Distribution.

Online Resources:
* *The Wrap* (www.thewrap.com)

Disc Distribution

There is another debate regarding the future of Disc Distribution, but because there remain standalone Disc rental options and Disc-By-Mail rental and sales outlets, Disc Distribution is definitely worth mentioning. Even as more and more media is available through Streaming or Digital Download, full-length Movies are rather large, cumbersome files, especially when stored on devices such as phones or tablets. Until the day comes when we can store seemingly endless amount of Movies on small or handheld devices (or until Streaming libraries become comprehensive), we will still have a need for physical media of some sort.

There are several options when choosing to put your Movie on Disc, and some added expenses as well if you are self-distributing. The first would be the creation of the Ultra HD (4K), Blu-ray (HD) and/or DVD master, using special Encoding and Disc Authoring Software. Most people have some version of this already on their personal computers, but if you're wanting to do it like the pros, then be sure to use the correct Software. This will ensure playback of your Discs across as many devices as possible, which will ultimately mean fewer merchandise returns due to technical issues. It's usually wise to hire somebody to do your Disc Authoring if you don't have any experience in this process. This is an opportunity to create a cool presentation for your Film and to show some extras like Motion Graphics, Deleted Scenes, Blooper Reels, Behind-The-Scenes slideshows, etc. This is also the stage at which foreign language Subtitles and Alternate Audio tracks are added, and any Copy Protection will be applied.

If you're remaining independent with your Distribution, the most important decision here is who to choose for your Disc Replication and how big of a batch you want to make—unless you choose an "On Demand" option. Getting quotes from various Disc Replication services is wise in order to learn which ones offer the best value, as lower overhead equals more potential profits. Some of them offer additional services such as Disc Authoring, Packaging and even Distribution options, which include getting listed on major online retail sites such as Amazon. This might be a great way to go if your Website isn't already generating steady traffic by now, as you may have Discs for sale but no way to reach potential customers.

Regarding physical Disc rentals, currently there are two main players: Redbox and Netflix. Redbox has kiosks inside or in front of grocery, retail and convenience stores all over the United States. Netflix is still offering the service/business model that made them famous in Disc-By-Mail (usually bundled with some level of their Streaming service). Both of these companies have different submission policies, and it's always best to read up on what the latest requirements are in terms of technical specifications, format, MPAA ratings and Movie Artwork.

Some of the technical requirements and overhead

costs associated with physical Disc-based media can be circumvented by going the route of Digital Distribution and Streaming.

Suggested Software:
- *Toast Titanium*
- *Sony Movie Studio*
- *Leawo Blu-ray Creator*

Online Resources:
- *YouTube* (www.youtube.com) – Encoding tutorials
- *CreateSpace* (www.createspace.com)
- *Disc Makers* (www.discmakers.com)
- *Redbox* (www.redbox.com)

Digital Distribution & Streaming

Digital Distribution, once thought of as a pipe dream, has become a reality thanks to increased internet bandwidths and the sophistication of playback devices. Companies such as Netflix have seen their dominant delivery methods go from Disc-By-Mail to Streaming in just over a decade thanks to the factors stated above.

There are some big players in this arena (Netflix, Hulu, Amazon Prime, iTunes and Google Play are some of the more familiar subscription services) but more independent-focused channels are popping up all the time. This has naturally lowered some of the barriers to entry, namely the cost of submission fees and the rigid standards in the selection of content.

Much like all the paths your Film can take, there are considerations to be made with each choice of Streaming outlet. I suggest going after the big outlets first and trying for a Netflix or iTunes. Then plan on falling back on some of the newer, smaller players if that doesn't work out. With Digital Distribution it's all about eyes on your Movie, and the larger the subscriber base, the more potential an outlet has to make your Movie a hit (or at least a "cult" favorite).

Something to be aware of is that there are services out there known as Aggregators that will submit your Film to several Streaming outlets at once. Using an Aggregator will save you time and hassle but at a cost.

The Streaming method does not generate a lot of profit, so don't plan on getting rich off your first Film if you end up distributing it this way. But if you have a Movie that sits atop the Most Watched list, even on a free Streaming format, it will garner some attention and could lead to a new gig or even your big break.

Don't get discouraged by rejection, because nothing you do is ever a wasted effort (even if you have some upset Investors to answer to). If your Movie still hasn't found its audience at this point in the process, it may at least help in securing Representation by becoming a showpiece for Agents and Managers.

Recommended Reading:
- *The Insider's Guide to Independent Film Distribution* by Stacey Parks

Online Resources:
- *Distribber* (www.distribber.com) – Aggregator service
- *Streaming Media* (www.streamingmedia.com)

Agents & Managers

At this point it's time to think about your next project, and how best to go about securing that. If your first Film doesn't lead to people beating down your door offering you a possible next gig, then it's time to reach out to Agents and Managers.

For clarity it's important to define in simple terms the difference between the two. An Agent is directly responsible for finding their Clients work while a Manager oversees the career paths of their Clients. For further clarification, a Personal Manager performs this role while a Business Manager serves in more of an Accountant role. Both take a cut from your salary; the percentages can vary, but 15% is standard.

Agents help package and submit your potential projects to the Studios, most of which won't read unsolicited material. Managers are key for their industry connections, and they sometimes even take on producing roles depending on the project and their personal interest in it.

Although technically you are hiring these people, any Agent or Manager worth their weight will be picky with regard to whom they take on as Clients. Having a Reel of your best and latest work ready will be the most important tool that you have, which is where your finished Movie comes in to play. Putting aside the financial successes or failures (which do matter to them because it will make you an easier or tougher sell), some are willing to take the risk if they see a certain level of quality in your work and believe in your future potential.

It can't hurt to attempt to contact some of the biggest Agencies first and again work your way down the list. Don't sit back and wait for a reply as many won't bother to respond. Keep sending out emails with a brief bio and link to your work. This is the time to talk yourself up without using the standard hyperbole since they have heard it all before. Find something unique about your Film, background or body of work and focus on that.

If you can differentiate yourself from the pack, an Agent might just pair you up with a project that has been sitting on their desk. Sometimes the key is just to continue working in this business as you're only as good as your last project. And that project had better be fairly recent, lest you risk being obsolete, or at the very least, out of practice.

Recommended Reading:
- *How to Manage Your Agent* by Chad Gervich
- *Career Opportunities in the Film Industry* by Fred Yager & Jan Yager

Online Resources:
- *Association of Talent Agents* (www.agentassociation.com)
- *IMDb Pro* (www.imdb.com/pro)
- *LinkedIn Premium* (www.premium.linkedin.com)
- *MovieMaker Magazine* (www.moviemaker.com)
- *The Hollywood Reporter* (www.hollywoodreporter.com)
- *Empire Magazine* (www.empireonline.com)

CONCLUSION

My intentions in writing this book were not to be the final word in all things related to Filmmaking. By no means are the methods prescribed here the only way to go about things; they are simply tips and insights accumulated over my 20+ years in the field.

If you are a beginning Filmmaker, I hope that you found this book to be an accessible, indispensable portal to the wealth of knowledge already out there. If you are an experienced Filmmaker, I hope that you found it to be an adequate, simple refresher for every stage of the process.

As you have seen in this book, even a "simplified" approach to Filmmaking can be a lot to take on at times. If you can remain focused on the task at hand, realizing how each piece fits together in relation to the next, then your chances of feeling overwhelmed will be lessened greatly.

I have always been of the mind that if a publication has even one helpful tip for doing what I love to do in a more efficient, professional way, then it is worth a read. I will consider this book a success on a personal level if I have been able to provide you with that, and I hope that my passion for the craft has shown through as well. One last piece of advice is universal–courtesy of the late, great Writer Ray Bradbury: "Love what you do and do what you love."

ABOUT THE AUTHOR

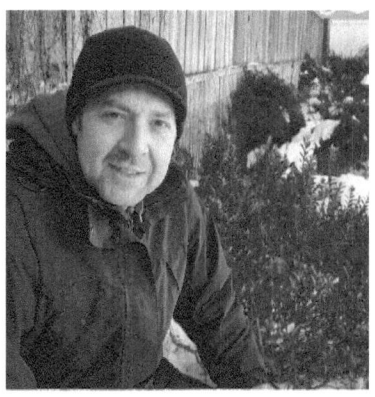

Flax Glor was born and raised in Santa Cruz, California,
where he spent his formative Filmmaking years
before moving to Hollywood to work on
large Studio Movies and Television Productions.

He has won awards for his
Short Films and Music Videos.
He is the founder of Smoothio Films
and now resides in the Portland, Oregon area.